access to history

Luther and the German Reformation 1517–55

THIRD EDITION

Russel Tarr

HODDER
EDUCATION
PART OF HACHETTE LIVRE UK

For Russell Charlesworth of Wolverhampton Grammar School, the best role-model a new teacher could wish for; and Dr. Clive Holmes of Lady Margaret Hall, Oxford University, whose infectious enthusiasm for Early Modern History was a genuine inspiration.

Study guides written by Angela Leonard (Edexcel), Geoff Woodward (OCR A) and Martin Jones (OCR B).

The Publishers would like to thank the following for permission to reproduce copyright material:

Photo credits
p.35 © Alinari Archives/Corbis; **p.117** © Arco Images GmbH/Alamy; **p121** © Bettmann/Corbis **p.103** Bildarchiv PreussischerKulturbesitz; **pp.50, 74** © The Bridgeman Art Library; **p.5** © Corbis; **p.12** Galleria degli Uffizi, Florence, Italy/The Bridgeman Art Library; **p.113** German Notes; **p.33** Getty Images; **p.132** © Gianni Dagli Orti/Corbis; **pp.7, 14, 27, 51, 70, 75, 77, 95** Mary Evans Picture Library; **p.144** Mary Evans/Aisa Media; **p.137** Mary Evans/Rue des Archives; **p.2** © NFP/photo Rolf von der Heydt; **p.21** © NFP*; **p.61** © The Gallery Collection/Corbis; **p.26** Time & Life Pictures/Getty Images; **p.142** © 2003 Topham Picturepoint; **p.114** © Werner Otto/VISUM/Still Pictures

Acknowledgements
p.42 Longman for an extract from A. Johnston, *The Protestant Reformation in Europe*, 1992; **p.123** R.W. Scribner, *The German Reformation*, 1986, Palgrave Macmillan reproduced with permission of Palgrave Macmillan; **p.145** Edexcel Limited for specimen material; **p.147** Longman for an extract from M. Rady, *The Emperor Charles V*, 1988

Every effort has been made to trace all copyright holders, but if any have been inadvertently overlooked the Publishers will be pleased to make the necessary arrangements at the first opportunity.

Hachette Livre UK's policy is to use papers that are natural, renewable and recyclable products and made from wood grown in sustainable forests. The logging and manufacturing processes are expected to conform to the environmental regulations of the country of origin.

Orders: please contact Bookpoint Ltd, 130 Milton Park, Abingdon, Oxon OX14 4SB. Telephone: (44) 01235 827720. Fax: (44) 01235 400454. Lines are open 9.00–5.00, Monday to Saturday, with a 24-hour message answering service. Visit our website at www.hoddereducation.co.uk

© Russel Tarr and Keith Randell © 1989
First published in 1989 by
Hodder Education,
Part of Hachette Livre UK
338 Euston Road
London NW1 3BH

Second edition published 2000

This third edition published 2008

Impression number 5 4 3 2 1
Year   2012 2011 2010 2009 2008

Cover photo shows a portrait of Martin Luther by Lucas Cranach the Elder, © The Gallery Collection/Corbis
Typeset in 10/12pt New Baskerville by GreenGate Publishing Services, Tonbridge
Printed in Malta

A catalogue record for this title is available from the British Library.

ISBN: 978 0340 965 917

Contents

Dedication

Keith Randell (1943–2002)

The *Access to History* series was conceived and developed by Keith, who created a series to 'cater for students as they are, not as we might wish them to be'. He leaves a living legacy of a series that for over 20 years has provided a trusted, stimulating and well-loved accompaniment to the post-16 study. Our aim with these new editions is to continue to offer students the best possible support for their studies.

Background to the Reformation

POINTS TO CONSIDER

In 1517, a German monk named Martin Luther produced a list of complaints against the Catholic Church – the famous *Ninety-five Theses* – which he then supposedly nailed onto the door of the castle church in Wittenberg. This was a brave action. In the sixteenth century the Christian Church was incredibly powerful; there was only one accepted Christian faith in the whole of Europe: Roman Catholicism, led by the Pope in Rome. Luther's protest started a train of events which ended with the division of the Christian Church. This famous event is often seen as the defining moment when the Christian Church divided into two rival factions – Protestant and Catholic – a state of affairs which continues to this day. This event, known as the Reformation, has been studied by more historians than almost any other topic. It has been a source of fascination for tens of thousands of students over several centuries and there is no sign of the interest abating.

This chapter introduces the Reformation by covering the following themes:

- Introduction: background to the Reformation
- The main disagreements between Lutherans and Catholics.

Key dates

1505	Luther abandoned a career in law and joined the priesthood
1516	Luther decided that 'faith alone' is what gets a soul into heaven and that therefore a great deal of Catholic belief and practice was a waste of time and energy
1517	Luther produced a list of complaints – the *Ninety-five Theses* – against Church abuses, especially the sale of indulgences
1521	Luther refused to back down before the Holy Roman Emperor, Charles V, at the Imperial Diet (Parliament) at Worms

1522/23	Ulrich von Hutten led the Knights' War, which used Luther's ideas to justify the violent seizure of church lands
1524–25	Thomas Müntzer led the Peasants' War, which used Luther's ideas to promote greater social justice
1529	Six Lutheran princes 'protested' at the second Diet of Speyer against the Catholic Church Luther published the *Large* and *Small Catechisms*
1546	Luther died at Wartburg Castle, Germany
1547	Battle of Mühlberg. Charles V defeated the Protestant Schmalkaldic League but failed to follow up the victory
1555	Charles V abdicated as Holy Roman Emperor. His successor agreed to the Peace of Augsburg, allowing each prince to decide the religion of his area

A still from the film *Luther*, showing Luther nailing up his *Ninety-five Theses* (complaints) against the Catholic Church, 1517. Is this the date the Reformation can be said to have started?

1 | Introduction: Background to the Reformation

Important concepts

'The Reformation'

Key question
What questionable
assumptions lie
behind the way in
which the Reformation
has traditionally been
studied?

Key terms

Protestant
A general term
referring to anyone
who 'protested'
against the Catholic
Church.

Reform
Change for the
better. The term
'Reformation' is
therefore one that
has inbuilt bias.

Propaganda
A form of
advertising designed
to persuade people
to view things in a
certain way.

Imperial Diet
The parliament of
the Holy Roman
Empire. This met in
various cities
around the Empire
during this period,
including Worms,
Augsburg and
Speyer.

At first sight, 'the Reformation' is a neutral concept used to describe
a historical process. The main features of this process are that large
numbers of people in Germany, Switzerland, Scandinavia, the
Netherlands and Great Britain turned their backs on Catholicism
and became members of independent **Protestant** churches.

However, we need to look more closely at the word
'Reformation'. The word '**reform**' immediately encourages us to
accept that these changes were for the better and were putting
right what was wrong. In reality, the fact that the concept has been
central to our study of sixteenth-century European history for
more than 200 years has been a great **propaganda** victory for
Luther's supporters.

'The Reformation' was not a term used either at the time or for
several generations afterwards. It was popularised in the
eighteenth century by Protestant historians in Germany who
assumed unquestioningly that 'the Reformation' had been a
process by which large numbers of strong Christians, unable to
accept the widespread abuses of the Catholic Church, had broken
away to form their own purified religion.

It is now far too late to attempt to abandon the concept, or even
to change its name – several centuries of calling it 'the Desertion'
might correct the balance – but we must at least try to be aware
that when we accept the idea of 'the Reformation' as a framework
for historical study, we are in danger of swallowing a considerable
number of questionable assumptions and value judgements at the
same time.

'Protestant'

Just as the word 'Reformation' can confuse our understanding of
the period, so too can the word 'Protestant'. This word was
originally used to describe the princes who formally sided with
Luther by 'protesting' against the Catholic Church at the **Imperial
Diet** (Parliament) of Speyer in 1529. As a result, 'Protestant' is
often used to mean the same thing as 'Lutheran'. This is
misleading. A 'Protestant' is a general term for anyone who
opposed the teachings of the Catholic Church. A 'Lutheran' is a
specific term for a Protestant who followed the teachings of Martin
Luther in particular. In other words, all Lutherans were
Protestants, but there were other types of Protestants too – for
example, Zwinglians, Calvinists and Radicals. As we shall see in
Chapter 6 the term 'Radicals' itself is a very general one covering a
whole range of other groups including Münsterites, Müntzerites,
Mennonites and Melchiorites.

It is important as you study the period to make sure that you are

Key date
Luther published the
Large and *Small
Catechisms*: 1529

as accurate as possible in your use of these words. Use the word
'Protestant' only when you wish to refer generally to any opponents
of the Catholic Church, otherwise you will be in danger of
assuming that all 'Protestants' believed in exactly the same things.

'Germany'

In 1500 'Germany' was a general term used to refer to a broad geographical area. The country that we today know as Germany did not come into existence until 1871. Before then, Germany belonged to the vast 'Holy Roman Empire' which covered much of central Europe. This was presided over by a **Holy Roman Emperor** who could summon a Diet whenever and in whichever city he liked. However, in practice the Holy Roman Emperor had limited powers. Firstly, his power was limited by the 'doctrine of the two swords'. This was the idea that the **Pope** should have full control of religion in the Empire (the 'religious sword') while the Emperor should involve himself only in politics (the '**secular** sword'). Secondly, the Empire was a fragmented collection of over 300 independent states, free towns and imperial cities which largely ran their own affairs. This meant that it was difficult for the Diet to reach any sort of agreement on important issues – and even more difficult to enforce its decisions if and when agreement was reached.

Important moments
The start of the Reformation

Every book on the Reformation needs to decide where to start the story. A general movement such as the Reformation cannot meaningfully be said to have started on a specific date, so there are several dates to choose from:

- 1505: Martin Luther was caught in a terrible thunderstorm. Terrified, he prayed to God promising to give up his law studies and devote his life to the Church if his life was spared. True to his word, he started training for the priesthood immediately afterwards.
- 1516: Luther had his 'tower experience'. He was working quietly in his study when he was struck by a phrase in the Bible which convinced him that the Catholic Church had completely misunderstood God's Word.
- 1517: Martin Luther produced his list of complaints against the Catholic Church – the famous *Ninety-five Theses* – which he then supposedly nailed onto the door of the castle church in Wittenberg.
- 1521: Luther was summoned by the Holy Roman Emperor to appear before the Imperial Diet at the German city of Worms. He was accused of heresy – the crime of challenging the beliefs of the Church. Luther stood before the Holy Roman Emperor, surrounded by cardinals, bishops and the leading princes of Germany. (The most senior figures in the Catholic Church were the Pope, the cardinals, the archbishops and the bishops. The Princes were the rulers of the German states.) He was presented with copies of his books and pamphlets and ordered to recant (withdraw) his arguments. Luther refused, saying, 'I cannot and I will not recant anything, for to go against conscience is neither right nor safe. Here I stand. I cannot do otherwise. God help me, Amen!'

Key terms

Holy Roman Emperor
The leader of the Holy Roman Empire, which was a loose confederation of states roughly equating to modern-day Germany, Austria, Hungary and the Netherlands.

Pope
The leader of the Catholic Church. This was Leo X when Luther's protest began.

Key question
Is it possible to establish when the Reformation started, became established, and ended?

Key term

Secular
To do with worldly, political affairs rather than those to do with religion.

Key dates

Luther abandoned a career in law and joined the priesthood: 1505

Luther decided that 'faith alone' is what gets a soul into heaven: 1516

Luther produced a list of complaints – the *Ninety-five Theses*: 1517

Luther refused to back down before the Holy Roman Emperor, Charles V, at the Imperial Diet at Worms: 1521

Profile: Martin Luther (1483–1546)

1483	– Luther was born the son of a wealthy silver miner. He had a strict upbringing and was pushed into studying law at Erfurt University
1505	– Caught in a thunderstorm, he pledged to become a monk if his life was spared
1507	– Ordained as a priest. He became increasingly uncomfortable with what he considered to be the mindless rituals of the Catholic Church
1516	– Luther's 'tower experience': reading the Bible, Luther was struck by the phrase 'The righteous shall live by faith'. For him, this meant that salvation can only be assured 'by faith alone' (*sola fide*)
1517	– Luther pinned *Ninety-five Theses* against Church abuses on the door of the university church at Wittenberg
1520	– Pope Leo X excommunicated Luther
1521	– The Diet of Worms: Luther appeared before Emperor Charles V but refused to recant. Luther was outlawed and his works were banned
1521	– Luther was 'kidnapped' by his own supporters and 'imprisoned' for his own protection in Wartburg Castle by Frederick of Saxony
1525	– Luther, a former monk, married Catherine von Bora, a former nun
1525–27	– A number of German princes converted to Lutheranism, including the Duke of Prussia, the Duke of Hesse and the Elector of Saxony
1546	– Luther died in Wartburg Castle; his last years were spent improving his translation of the Bible into German

Martin Luther is the towering figure of the German Reformation. Trained as a lawyer, he switched over to the priesthood after surviving a terrifying thunderstorm. His logical, legal mind found little spiritual comfort in the rituals of the Catholic Church and he spent a lot of time reading the Bible to get closer to God. During one of these study periods in 1516 he came across the phrase 'The righteous shall live by faith' in St Paul's Epistle to the Romans. For Luther, this meant that faith alone (in Latin, *sola fide*) was what got a soul into heaven – not pilgrimages, charitable donations, worship of saints or any other of those 'good works' which the Catholic Church promoted. Luther was completely inspired by this insight, later recalling that 'I felt that I was altogether born again and had entered paradise itself through open gates'.

In 1517, the Indulgences Controversy stung Luther into action. Johann Tetzel was wandering around Germany selling 'indulgences' from the Pope to raise money for the rebuilding of St Peter's Church in Rome. People who bought these documents were promised forgiveness for their sins and immediate entry into heaven when they died. For Luther, this was the clearest evidence yet that the Catholic Church had become corrupt. He pinned up a list of complaints against Church abuses – the *Ninety-five Theses* – on the church door at Wittenberg University.

The Catholic Church first tried to terrify Luther into submission by summoning him to meet the fearsome Cardinal Cajetan. When this failed, the Church tried to persuade Luther that he was wrong by engaging him in a head-to-head debate with Johann Eck. Luther, however, defended his idea of *sola fide* convincingly. Not only that, he went even further by saying that the Bible alone (*sola scriptura*) should be consulted to decide which rituals, procedures and officers of the Church were really necessary. On this basis, Luther not only swept away a large number of beliefs and sacraments of the Catholic Church which had developed over the centuries, but also rejected the authority of the Pope himself.

The Church then issued Luther with a papal bull (proclamation) which excommunicated him – in other words, condemned him to hell. Luther responded by publicly burning the bull and writing pamphlets circulated by printing presses all over Europe. First, *The Babylonish Captivity of the Church* denied the holiness of four sacraments and stated that, as a consequence of *sola fide*, free will 'is utterly smashed to pieces'. *The Liberty of a Christian Man* stresses that good works reflect, but do not in themselves bestow, Grace. *The Address to the Christian Nobility* defines the priesthood of all believers, stresses the leadership role of princes and rejects papal abuses. The Holy Roman Emperor was then called upon by the Pope to bring Luther under control. At the Imperial Diet (parliament) at Worms, Luther famously stood firm with the famous words 'Here I stand. I cannot do otherwise. So help me God. Amen.' From this point on, Luther was outlawed in the Empire as well as excommunicated from the Church. This placed him in very real personal danger. For his own safety, his supporters kidnapped him and hid him away at Wartburg Castle under the protection of Frederick of Saxony. From this point the leadership of the Reformation passed into the hands of others. Luther married, raised a family of six children and devoted much of his time to producing a German translation of the Bible.

Luther was a complex character whose views were not always followed through consistently. On the one hand he was an inspired and inspiring religious revolutionary. He stressed the power of individuals to control their own destinies. He rejected the authority of the Church and the state to determine the fate of people's souls. He was prepared to risk his life by challenging the Pope and the Holy Roman Emperor rather than compromise his religious convictions. By doing this, he spearheaded a movement which shattered the power of the Church.

On the other hand, Luther was a conservative in every other way. He failed to see why his radical religious ideas should have social and political implications. The Imperial Knights used Luther's ideas as an excuse to attack the lands of the Archbishop of Trier and Luther was shocked. When the peasants rose up in revolt demanding greater social equality on the Lutheran basis that all men were equal before God, Luther was appalled. He even produced a pamphlet entitled *Against the Murdering, Thieving Hordes of Peasants* which encouraged the government to 'smite and slay' the rebels. Thousands of peasants were killed in the campaign which followed and Luther's reputation as a champion of the ordinary people never recovered from this episode.

Martin Luther at the Diet of Worms, 1521. What impression of Luther does the artist seek to create in this painting?

The establishment of the Reformation

It is also difficult to pin down the date on which Luther's individual protest turned into a powerful movement. Although it started as one man's protest against the Catholic Church, Martin Luther's campaign quickly gathered momentum. Within a few years it had attracted support from every class of society within the Holy Roman Empire – from princes and **Imperial Knights** down to lowly peasants. Luther himself was alarmed by the way in which the movement he had started quickly spiralled out of his control.

- The date at which the Reformation became established is perhaps 1522, when the 'Knights' War' saw a group of Imperial Knights led by Ulrich von Hutten latch onto the nationalistic element of Luther's message.
- Alternatively, we could suggest it was 1524, when the 'Peasants' War' saw the lower classes of society demand greater social justice on the basis that Luther had shown that all men were equal before the eyes of God.
- Another date would be 1529: it was in this year that a group of German princes formally adopted Lutheranism after making their 'protest' against the Catholic Church at the Diet of Speyer.

The end of the Reformation

Similar problems arise over settling the end date for the Reformation in Germany:

- 1546: Luther, the man who started the Reformation, died.
- 1547: Emperor Charles V defeated the Protestants at the Battle of Mühlberg but failed to crush their religion and finally realised that he would never do so.
- 1555: The Peace of Augsburg accepted that the religion of each state within Germany – Lutheran or Catholic – was to be decided by its ruler, not by the Holy Roman Emperor.

However, even at this point the story was far from over: Catholic groups such as the Jesuits, and Protestant groups such as the Calvinists, would continue the Reformation of religion for many more years to come.

The key debate

There is much lively debate between historians over the question:

> What date period should be used in a study of the Reformation?

Historians divide into three main camps with regard to this issue.

Some historians argue that the period 1517–55 marked a truly decisive break with the past: Martin Luther formulated revolutionary religious ideas that had an immediate impact. This viewpoint was championed by Luther's early followers such as Matthias Flacius Illyricus (1520–75); it has continued to be supported by the great biographers of Luther such as Roland Bainton as well as religious historians such as Wilfried Joest and Oswald Bayer.

Key term

Imperial Knights
A class of minor nobles in the Holy Roman Empire.

Key dates

Ulrich von Hutten led the Knights' War, which used Luther's ideas to justify the violent seizure of church lands: 1522/23

Six Lutheran princes 'protested' at the second Diet of Speyer against the Catholic Church: 1529

Luther died at Warburg Castle, Germany: 1546

Key dates

Battle of Mühlberg: Charles V defeated the Protestant Schmalkaldic League but failed to crush Protestantism: 1547

Peace of Augsburg: Charles V accepted that the religious divisions in the Empire were permanent. He abdicated as Holy Roman Emperor shortly afterwards: 1555

Other historians argue that, from a religious standpoint, the start date of the Reformation needs to be much earlier than 1517. They maintain that Luther's theology merely consolidated ideas which had been developing within and outside of the Catholic Church since the Middle Ages. This view is supported not only by Ernst Troeltsch but also by Heiko Oberman, who describes Lutheranism as 'the harvest of medieval theology'.

A final group of historians suggests that, in political and social terms, the end date of the Reformation needs to be much later than 1555. Their view is that Luther's ideas did not have any major impact on ordinary people until the second half of the sixteenth century, when a new generation of reformers focused on the creation of Church institutions and practices which helped to create distinct 'national' identities. The two historians most closely associated with this position are Heinz Schilling and Wolfgang Reinhard.

Some key books in the debate:
Roland Bainton, *Here I Stand: A Life of Martin Luther*, reprint of 1950 edition (Penguin, 1995).
Heiko A. Oberman, *Luther: Man between God and the Devil* (Image, 1989)
Heinz Schilling, *Religion, Political Culture and the Emergence of Early Modern Society* (Brill, 1992)

The key individual

Key question
What is the danger of overstating Martin Luther's personal importance in events?

Luther is undoubtedly the towering figure of the German Reformation and so it is sensible to focus on his personality and actions when studying the period. Without this Luther-centred approach it is very difficult to make any sense of the many conflicting interpretations that surround the subject. But there are disadvantages to this approach.

Firstly, a whole mythology has grown up around Luther's life and it is very difficult to disentangle fact from fiction. For example, Luther is supposed to have dramatically nailed up a list of 95 complaints upon the church door in Wittenberg – but he never claimed to have done so. Similiarly, at the Imperial Diet (parliament) at Worms there is no evidence that he actually delivered the famous words 'Here I stand. I cannot do otherwise. So help me God. Amen.' These two events were probably manufactured after the events to provide dramatic interest to the story by people eager to generate sympathy for Luther's ideas.

Secondly, it is vital to remember that, although Luther was highly important, other people also had a major effect on what happened. Luther came from a long line of influential critics of the Catholic Church and in this sense he can be seen as part of a process rather than as the sole originator of the Reformation. Moreover, without the help of key figures such as Frederick of Saxony (see Chapter 2) and Philipp Melanchthon (see Chapter 7), Luther's challenge to the Church could easily have failed as had the others that went before it. Finally, Luther quickly became aware that he could not easily control the Reformation he had helped to start. By questioning the beliefs of the Catholic Church, he inadvertently challenged the political and social system that had been built upon them. This helps to underline the point that the German Reformation was not purely and simply defined by Luther and Lutheranism.

Thirdly, we could argue that any approach which explains the cause of events by focusing on a handful of individuals is far too superficial. This approach, followed by early supporters of Luther such as Matthias Flacius Illyricus (1520–75), is sometimes described as the 'Great Man' theory of history and was at its most popular a century or so ago. Although it provides us with a dramatic narrative, this approach is now out of favour. For example, **Marxist** historians such as Steinmetz argue that individuals are the product of economic circumstances, while **Annales** historians such as Fernand Braudel argue that these economic circumstances are the product of much deeper geographical and climatic factors.

So recent historians are much more inclined to see Luther as the 'trigger' in a chain of explosive political, religious, social and economic circumstances which had been building up for hundreds of years across the whole of Europe. Accepting this point, it is argued, will allow us to formulate meaningful answers to questions such as: 'Why did the Reformation take place where and when it did?', 'Why did it spread so widely and so rapidly?' and 'What effect did it have on the lives of the people?'

Key terms

Marxist
A follower of Karl Marx, a highly influential nineteenth-century historian and philosopher who saw economic factors as being the main driving force in history.

Annales
A school of historians, based in France, who see geographical and climatic conditions as being the main driving force in history.

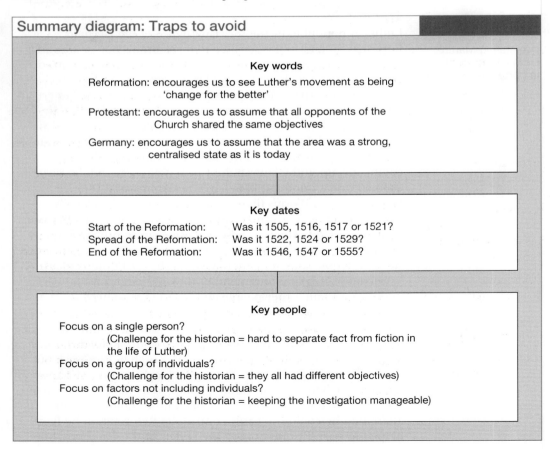

Summary diagram: Traps to avoid

Key words

Reformation: encourages us to see Luther's movement as being 'change for the better'

Protestant: encourages us to assume that all opponents of the Church shared the same objectives

Germany: encourages us to assume that the area was a strong, centralised state as it is today

Key dates

Start of the Reformation: Was it 1505, 1516, 1517 or 1521?
Spread of the Reformation: Was it 1522, 1524 or 1529?
End of the Reformation: Was it 1546, 1547 or 1555?

Key people

Focus on a single person?
  (Challenge for the historian = hard to separate fact from fiction in the life of Luther)
Focus on a group of individuals?
  (Challenge for the historian = they all had different objectives)
Focus on factors not including individuals?
  (Challenge for the historian = keeping the investigation manageable)

Key question
What were the key disagreements between Lutherans and Catholics?

Key terms

Grace
Merit in the eyes of God. A 'state of Grace' is a condition of perfection which allows a soul to enter into heaven.

Justification
The process by which a soul justifies (explains) why it is worthy of entering heaven.

Original sin
The 'first crime' – in the Old Testament, Adam and Eve were thrown out of the garden of Eden when Eve disobeyed God by eating the 'forbidden fruit' (an apple).

Pilgrimages
Journies to holy places such as Jerusalem. Catholics regard pilgrimages as an example of 'good works'.

Chantries
Places where monks would say prayers for souls to help them get into heaven. Many Catholics left money to chantries in their wills.

2 | The Main Disagreements between Lutherans and Catholics

This book is mainly concerned with the causes, the course and the consequences of the Reformation. However, it is not possible to understand the personalities, concepts and events of the period without a good basic understanding of what Lutherans and Catholics actually argued about.

Justification

Lutherans and Catholics agreed that to enter heaven a soul must 'justify' itself before God. Once justified the soul enters into a state of **Grace** and enters the gates of paradise. Both groups also agreed that the process of **justification** was no easy matter, because mankind is tainted with the **original sin** of Adam and Eve. They also agreed that Christ's death on the cross created a 'store' of Grace which God used to save people from the flames of hell. The key disagreement was over how God chose to use that store of Grace.

The Catholic view: free will/justification by works

The Catholic view was that God puts the store of Grace at our disposal. We earn Grace by doing 'good works' – for example by giving to charity and going on **pilgrimages**. In other words, God gives us free will to make our own way to heaven or hell. A connected idea was that the saints, because of their pure lives, went into heaven with a surplus of Grace which they could bestow upon deserving souls as they saw fit. From this came Catholic devotion to particular saints – most notably to the Virgin Mary, but also in the form of pilgrimages to shrines such as that of St Thomas Becket (an archbishop murdered after defending the Church against the king) at Canterbury. This store of Grace was also at the disposal of the Pope, who could grant 'indulgences' to members of his Church, which were documents promising forgiveness for sins. Even after death, Catholics could continue doing 'good works'. Catholics believed that before entering heaven, most souls went to purgatory – a halfway house between heaven and hell where they would be purified. In their wills, many Catholics therefore left money to **chantries**, where monks spent their time praying for the souls of their benefactors to help them get out of purgatory and into heaven more quickly. Henry VII of England left a small fortune to chantries in this way.

This theory of justification provided a clear and stable framework for an uneducated population and stressed the free will of all men to control their destinies. Nevertheless, whilst the Church stressed that good works were meaningless without real faith, some people took the view that the rich could almost buy their way into heaven – especially when many popes lived lavish lifestyles.

Profile: Pope Leo X (1475–1521)

1475	– Born as Giovanni de Medici, the second son of Lorenzo 'the Magnificent', the most famous ruler of the Florentine Republic
1489	– Made a cardinal at the age of 14 due to his family connections
1489–91	– Studied theology at the University of Pisa
1513	– Became pope and adopted the title Leo X
1513–17	– Preoccupied with the Italian Wars; religious matters are neglected
1518	– Issued a bull confirming that indulgences had the power to bestow saving Grace
1519	– Failed to persuade Frederick of Saxony to stand for election as Holy Roman Emperor
1520	– Issued a bull excommunicating Martin Luther from the Catholic Church
1521	– Awarded the title 'Defender of the Faith' to King Henry VIII of England, who had written a book attacking Luther's ideas
1521	– Died suddenly of malaria

Leo X was pope when Martin Luther made his protest against the Church. For Protestants at the time and many historians since, Leo embodies the shameless corruption and extravagance of the Catholic Church on the eve of the Reformation. More recently, however, historians have been less willing to accept this simple interpretation, arguing that while Pope Leo X was undoubtedly a flawed character, he was substantially less corrupt than many of the popes that had preceded him.

When he became pope, Leo X reportedly said to his brother Giuliano: 'Since God has given us the papacy, let us enjoy it.' The Venetian ambassador who first related this story was a hostile witness, but it was widely repeated and this says a lot about the Pope's reputation as a pleasure-seeker. His extravagance knew no bounds: he enjoyed travelling around Rome at the head of lavish parades which featured jesters, panthers and Hanno, his pet white elephant. To fund his lifestyle he borrowed large sums from foreign bankers, auctioned Church offices and sold indulgences.

Leo also had the reputation of being more interested in politics than in religion. As a member of the wealthy Medici family of Florence, he was frequently embroiled in the Italian Wars which plagued the area for most of his life. He thought nothing of switching between different sides during the conflict when it served his own interests and of using his power and wealth as pope to further his own family's interests. In an example which illustrates both his unpopularity and his greed, he imposed heavy fines on a group of cardinals whom he accused of plotting to have him murdered.

However, more recent studies have presented a more sympathetic view of Leo X and have argued that many of the slurs against Pope Leo X are unfair. True, Leo was extravagant in his spending; however, as the head of a Church which placed emphasis on the importance of ceremonies and spectacles for inspiring awe and wonder, this was arguably money well spent. Moreover, Leo X donated large amounts of money to charity: each year, he lavished more than 6000 ducats in alms as well as giving large sums to hospitals and retirement homes.

Moreover, Pope Leo X was a great sponsor of the arts and education. He increased the salaries of professors at the University of Rome and thereby attracted distinguished teachers from all over Europe. He sponsored the great artist Raphael and appointed him to safeguard the classical antiquities around Rome. A report of the Venetian ambassador Marino Giorgi in 1517 presents a similarly positive picture: 'The Pope is a good-natured and extremely free-hearted man, who avoids every difficult situation and above all wants peace; he would not undertake a war himself unless his own personal interests were involved; he loves learning; of canon law and literature he possesses remarkable knowledge; he is, moreover, a very excellent musician.'

Lutherans: predestination/justification by faith alone (*sola fide*)

Luther felt the Catholic stress on good works had led people to become rather lazy in their devotion to God. He also felt that worship of saints distracted people from the teachings of Jesus Christ and importance of His sacrifice on the cross. Lutherans believed that God did not put the store of Grace created by that sacrifice at our disposal. Instead, He had already used it to predestine a random proportion of mankind ('**the Elect**') to be saved, whilst the rest ('**the Damned**') would deservedly perish in the flames of hell. There was no such place as purgatory – which after all was not mentioned anywhere in the Bible – and no number of good works could change the fate which God had already decided for us. Therefore, the purpose of our lives should be to search within ourselves for the faith in God's teachings which is the hallmark of the Elect. Superficially this seems to remove all moral responsibility – why bother leading a virtuous life if we don't get rewarded for it? Luther's response was that only the Damned would think in such cynical terms – good works might not bestow Grace in themselves, but they were the natural

Key terms

'The Elect'
The group of people who had been marked out by God as being destined for heaven.

'The Damned'
People whose souls were destined to go to hell.

product of someone who possessed true faith. In other words, good deeds were the hallmark of the Elect, whilst sin was the hallmark of the Damned.

The Lutheran view of justification ingeniously encouraged virtuous living whilst simultaneously denying the free will at the heart of Catholicism. On the other hand, the stress on personal faith and inner reflection compared with unquestioning obedience to the Pope threatened to fragment the entire Church and, by implication, all of the political and social structures built upon it.

A sinner in purgatory purges his wickedness but hopes for better things as one of his companions who has served her term is released by an angel. Why did Luther argue that purgatory did not exist and that many other Catholic beliefs were incorrect?

The Bible
Catholics: Latin Vulgate

The Catholic demand for obedience to the Pope required one centrally controlled Biblical text. This text, called the **Vulgate**, was in Latin – partly because this was the international language of diplomacy of the time, but also because this ensured that it could not be read by the **laity**. The **papacy** argued that this was important to avoid misinterpretations and confusion. Critics suggested that it was just a way of preserving the power of the Church by preventing people from thinking for themselves.

Lutherans: vernacular versions

The Lutheran stress on individual reflection led to the production of Bibles in the **vernacular** – that is, the language of the ordinary people of a particular nation or region. Luther said that only by reference to scripture alone (*sola scriptura*) could each person decide whether they had faith and were therefore among the Elect. The down side was that people often formed different interpretations of what the Bible meant on key issues. Also, those who could not read were left feeling lost and abandoned as different preachers told them different things. Some reformers such as Caspar von Schwenkfeld and Andreas von Karlstadt even rejected the Bible altogether as a 'paper Pope' and instead advocated direct communication with the Holy Spirit through prayer. These reformers were called 'spiritualists' and are examined in more detail in Chapter 6.

The priesthood
Catholics: separate, centralised clergy

For Catholics, the clergy was of central importance. Grace was earned by the stable framework of good works defined by the Church through a standard Latin Bible. So, it followed that the priesthood needed to be highly educated, able to read Latin, knowledgeable about the complexities of Church beliefs and able to express them clearly and accurately to the people. With their exclusive access to the Bible, the priesthood guided its flock through their lives and towards heaven. Priests were 'special' – a halfway house between God and the people. It was only through the sacraments, administered by the priests, that sanctifying Grace could be obtained. From this came the idea of a celibate clergy and monasteries where holy men could cut themselves off from the corruption of the everyday world. It also meant a complex church hierarchy including a pope, cardinals, bishops and parish priests. This provided stability and order to society, but it also created tension since priests could easily abuse their power for financial gain.

Lutherans' decentralised 'priesthood of all believers'

The Lutheran belief in individual reflection, using a vernacular Bible, made much of the clergy redundant. Luther instead advocated a 'priesthood of all believers' – no one knows or can influence who is damned and who is saved, so all men are equal and have the potential to become priests. The implications of this were enormous. If the clergy was just as likely to be damned as everyone else, then monasteries, a celibate clergy and the Pope himself were pointless.

Luther attempted to moderate the implications of this idea by supporting a 'Magisterial Reformation', a process of change led by the ruling class rather than the mob. Nevertheless, radical reformers such as Thomas Müntzer spearheaded a 'popular Reformation', arguing that if we are all equal before God then there is no divine reason why the peasants should be downtrodden – indeed, as the largest class in society they should lead the movement. Luther was appalled by this application of his religious ideas to social affairs. When the peasants rose up in open revolt in 1524 (see Chapter 4), Luther wrote his notorious pamphlet *Against the Murdering, Thieving Hordes of Peasants* – but this had little impact on the course of events.

Ceremonies and appearances

Catholics

With its structured beliefs, a strict hierarchy and a conviction that charitable donations to the Church could help a soul into heaven, the Catholic Church became incredibly wealthy and powerful. Inside a typical church, one would find numerous visual aids designed to inspire and to teach – images of Christ's mother, the Virgin Mary; murals (wall paintings) of heaven, hell and purgatory; stories from the lives of those saints who might be persuaded to give members of the congregation some of their Grace. Catholic devotion to the saints, combined with the idea of good works, also led to the building of shrines at certain holy sites which quickly attracted pilgrims from far and wide. The more visually inspiring they were, the greater the number of pilgrims who visited and donated to their 'upkeep'. The shrine of **St Thomas Becket** at Canterbury had so many treasures that Henry VIII had to use scores of wagons to bring the loot to London.

Central to the ritual and theatre of the Catholic Church were the seven **sacraments**, each one carried out by a priest:

- baptism: temporary admission of an infant into the Church
- penance: confession of sins and their forgiveness
- the Eucharist: drinking of wine which has been transformed into the blood of Christ

---

Key term

Sola scriptura
'By scripture alone' – the idea that any church beliefs and practices not outlined in the Bible did not help a soul enter heaven.

Key date

Thomas Müntzer led the Peasants' War, which used Luther's ideas to promote greater social justice: 1524–25

Key question
How did Catholics and Lutherans disagree about ceremonies and appearances within the Church?

Key figure

St Thomas Becket
An archbishop of Canterbury who was murdered after defending the Church against the King of England.

Key term

Sacraments
The central rituals of the Catholic Church, administered by a priest, which were essential for salvation.

- confirmation: permanent admission of an adult into the Church
- marriage: union of two people with the aim of producing children
- ordination: commitment of a person to pursue a career in the Church
- last rites: final blessing and forgiveness of sins before death.

These provided 'cradle to the grave' spiritual healthcare, a framework for life that Catholics found deeply reassuring. The sacraments also reinforced the status of the 'elite' clergy by making it clear that these sacraments could only help people into heaven if carried out by a priest.

Lutherans

For Lutherans, the solemn rituals and visual magnificence of the Catholic Church merely distracted attention from the sacrifice of Christ and the centrality of the Bible. Getting into heaven would require a soul to have faith; the only way to discover that faith was through the Bible; and anything that detracted from the Bible was therefore to be discouraged. This emphasis on inward reflection regarding God's message meant that Lutheran churches were plain and simple. Nothing should distract attention from the Bible and the preacher. Rituals, images and financial donations to the Church were irrelevant at best, godless at worst. Only those things with a clear Biblical basis could hold a central place in the rituals of the Church. As a result, only three sacraments (baptism, penance and the Eucharist) were to be kept. Even they were to be interpreted in new terms – the sacrament of penance should emphasise 'being penitent' (justification by faith) rather than 'doing penance' (justification by good works). The sacrament of the Eucharist needed to involve the congregation partaking of both the bread and the wine (priesthood of all believers).

Summary diagram: Early differences between Protestants and Catholics

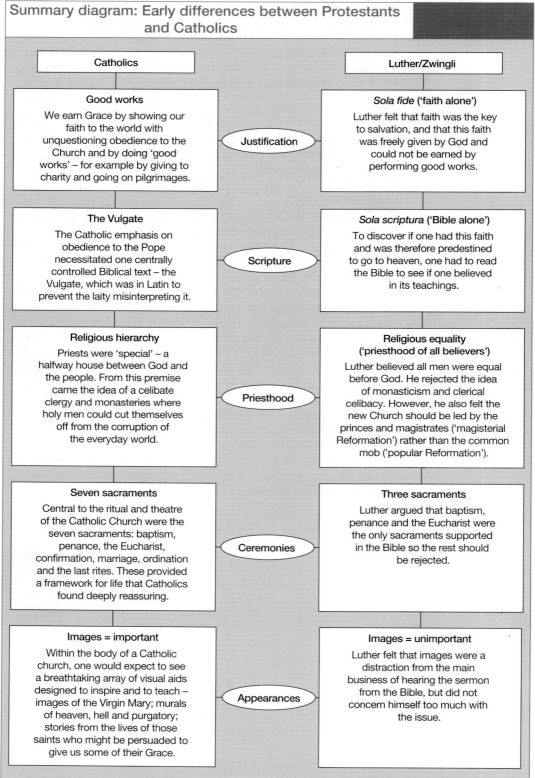

Catholics	Luther/Zwingli

Good works

We earn Grace by showing our faith to the world with unquestioning obedience to the Church and by doing 'good works' – for example by giving to charity and going on pilgrimages.

— Justification —

Sola fide ('faith alone')

Luther felt that faith was the key to salvation, and that this faith was freely given by God and could not be earned by performing good works.

The Vulgate

The Catholic emphasis on obedience to the Pope necessitated one centrally controlled Biblical text – the Vulgate, which was in Latin to prevent the laity misinterpreting it.

— Scripture —

Sola scriptura ('Bible alone')

To discover if one had this faith and was therefore predestined to go to heaven, one had to read the Bible to see if one believed in its teachings.

Religious hierarchy

Priests were 'special' – a halfway house between God and the people. From this premise came the idea of a celibate clergy and monasteries where holy men could cut themselves off from the corruption of the everyday world.

— Priesthood —

Religious equality ('priesthood of all believers')

Luther believed all men were equal before God. He rejected the idea of monasticism and clerical celibacy. However, he also felt the new Church should be led by the princes and magistrates ('magisterial Reformation') rather than the common mob ('popular Reformation').

Seven sacraments

Central to the ritual and theatre of the Catholic Church were the seven sacraments: baptism, penance, the Eucharist, confirmation, marriage, ordination and the last rites. These provided a framework for life that Catholics found deeply reassuring.

— Ceremonies —

Three sacraments

Luther argued that baptism, penance and the Eucharist were the only sacraments supported in the Bible so the rest should be rejected.

Images = important

Within the body of a Catholic church, one would expect to see a breathtaking array of visual aids designed to inspire and to teach – images of the Virgin Mary; murals of heaven, hell and purgatory; stories from the lives of those saints who might be persuaded to give us some of their Grace.

— Appearances —

Images = unimportant

Luther felt that images were a distraction from the main business of hearing the sermon from the Bible, but did not concern himself too much with the issue.

Key question
In what ways did
Catholics and
Lutherans share a
common outlook?

3 | The Common Ground of Intolerance between Protestants and Catholics

For Luther, the Catholic notion of free will meant little more than the free will to follow mindlessly the teachings of the Catholic Church or to burn in hell. In his view, the intellectual vitality which characterised the early Church had been replaced by rituals and mindless obedience. Luther rejected justification by works and therefore the idea that we have free will to forge our own path into heaven. Only by denying free will could he encourage people to look within themselves to discover if they were one of the Elect. Both Catholics and Protestants had to deal in absolutes, so their disagreements quickly appeared insurmountable. Soon, the only thing they appeared to have in common was intolerance – not only of each other, but of the Radicals (covered in Chapter 6), who were attacked with a violence out of all proportion to their numbers and influence.

2 Luther's Revolt

POINTS TO CONSIDER
In 2003 Martin Luther was the subject of a Hollywood film with Joseph Fiennes in the starring role. This choice of subject matter is hardly surprising. In a study of the German Reformation, we find all the ingredients required for a good story. There is a larger-than-life character, Martin Luther, a monk who dedicates his life to God after being saved from a dramatic thunderstorm. He takes the vow of obedience but, after a blinding revelation, decides to rebel against the Head of the Church. There is plenty of corruption in high places, accompanied by evidence of irregular sexual practices. There are possibilities to explore popular themes – the weak struggling successfully against the strong; the good overcoming the bad; or the darkness of ignorance being dispelled by the light of understanding. Great care is needed to avoid the dangers of viewing the events with the perspective of the twentieth century or through the filter of one's own prejudices.

This chapter focuses on the personality, life and career of Martin Luther. It describes the stages by which he became a rebel against the authority of the Church. It also explains the motives of Luther and of the Pope for acting as they did.

The chapter is structured in the following manner:

- Introduction: the dangers of bias
- Towards *sola fide*: Luther's ideas up to 1517
- Luther's reasons for opposing the Church: the Indulgences Controversy
- The spread of the *Ninety-five Theses*
- Attempts to silence Luther, 1517–21
- Towards *sola scriptura*: Luther's ideas 1517–21.

Key dates

1511	Luther assumed a lecturing post at Wittenberg University
1516	Luther developed the idea of *sola fide* following his 'tower experience'

1517	Luther produced a list of complaints – the *Ninety-five Theses* – against Church abuses, especially the sale of indulgences
1518	Luther was summoned to Augsburg and threatened by Cardinal Cajetan
1519	Luther was summoned to Leipzig and questioned by Johann Eck
1519	Luther developed the idea of *sola scriptura* following his debate with Johann Eck
1520	Luther was excommunicated by Pope Leo X
1521 April	Luther was outlawed by Emperor CharlesV at the Diet of Worms for refusing to withdraw his complaints against the Church
1521 May	Luther was 'kidnapped' by his own supporters for his own protection and hidden by Frederick the Wise at Wartburg Castle

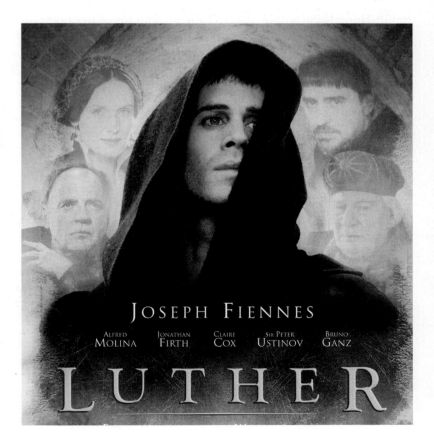

The DVD cover for the film *Luther*, produced in 2003. Which key events in Luther's life would come across particularly well on the big screen?

1 | Introduction: The Dangers of Bias

Religious bias

Everybody approaches the Reformation with some sort of bias. For those brought up in an active Christian tradition there is a side to identify with – either Catholic or Protestant – even before any evidence is studied. However hard the student or historian who has been brought up in contact with organised Christian religion tries to be neutral, there are likely to be times when a basic assumption that one side or the other is fundamentally in the right will show through. Very often these judgements are painfully obvious. So it is possible to identify a 'Catholic school' and a 'Protestant school' of historians who have studied Martin Luther, as can be seen when you read the 'key debates' which appear throughout this book.

Political bias

Even those historians who do not belong to one of these two schools are not automatically more reliable just because their prejudices are less obvious. It is no easier for the non-Christian, the **agnostic** or the **atheist**, to study the Reformation from a neutral position. Even if there is no inbuilt religious prejudice to overcome, there is likely to be a natural inclination for the radical to favour the idealistic rebel and for the conservative to favour the pragmatic forces of established authority. In no book on the Reformation is the author able to write without his or her point of view playing a part. Readers studying Martin Luther should try to identify the opinion of each author, and then decide how far to accept the interpretation put forward. There are no exceptions to this rule – not even the present volume.

Key question
Why is it important to recognise the point of view you already hold when you begin studying Luther and the German Reformation?

Agnostic
Someone who refuses either to accept or to deny the existence of God.

Atheist
Someone who does not believe in the existence of God.

Key terms

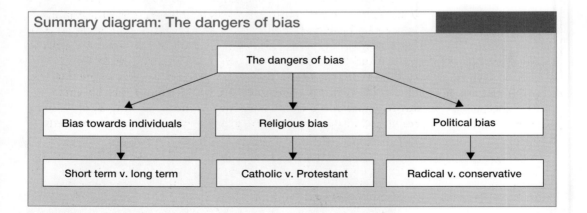

Summary diagram: The dangers of bias

The dangers of bias

- Bias towards individuals
  - Short term v. long term
- Religious bias
  - Catholic v. Protestant
- Political bias
  - Radical v. conservative

Christendom
The territories whose official religion was Christianity.

Schism
A division or a split within a group or an organisation.

Electoral Saxony
The state within the Holy Roman Empire where Luther began his protest. A generation earlier the state of Saxony had been divided in two – electoral Saxony ruled over by an elector, and ducal Saxony ruled over by a duke.

Holy relics
Artefacts from the life of a saint – bones, hair, clothing and so on – which were felt by Catholics to have special powers to heal and bestow Grace.

Luther took up a lecturing post at Wittenberg University: 1511

Luther developed the idea of *sola fide*: 1516

Luther produced the *Ninety-five Theses*: 1517

2 | Towards *Sola Fide*: Luther's Ideas up to 1517

Between the years 1517 and 1521 the actions of Martin Luther (1483–1546) shook the foundations of the Catholic Church, and threatened to shatter the medieval concept of **Christendom**. After 1521 there was a real possibility that the 'Church united' would not survive. This situation was not the outcome of a pre-planned series of attacks that was designed to have this result. It was just that one thing led to another until eventually there was no going back, and the only way forward was **schism** (the division of the Church into several Churches). It was as much a matter of events controlling people as of people controlling events.

The *Ninety-five Theses*: timing

As with many major events in history, the beginnings of Luther's revolt against the Catholic Church were relatively trivial. Legend has it that on the eve of All Saints' Day, 31 October 1517, he pinned the *Ninety-five Theses* against the sale of indulgences to the door of the main church in Wittenberg, the capital of **electoral Saxony**. The theses were in Latin and were intended to invite academic debate on the subject. The fact that they were pinned to the church door was not unusual. This was an accepted way of 'going public' with a point of view in the days before newspapers and television. What was a little unusual was the timing of the action. The *Ninety-five Theses* appeared just a few hours before the one day in the year on which the Elector of Saxony sold indulgences to those who visited his famous collection of **holy relics**. Luther clearly intended his arguments to receive wide publicity.

The *Ninety-five Theses*: main ideas

At this time Luther was a professor at the recently founded University of Wittenberg. His particular interest was the Bible, about which he had been lecturing at the university since he had been sent there in 1511. Like many academics of his time, Luther was a monk and as such was compelled to serve where his superiors directed him. But he was in no way a dry intellectual like so many of his colleagues. He was driven by a remarkably strong inner force which gave him no peace as long as he remained in doubt about the exact way in which God decided who should enter heaven. This force had been the most important influence in his life ever since he had become a monk at the age of 21 following a promise he had made to St Anne, his patron saint (a holy figure associated with a particular trade), for protecting him when caught in a frightening thunderstorm.

In his early years Luther had accepted the Church's teaching that salvation was to be gained by being 'sin-free' at the time of death. This could be assured by carrying out good works in life which could counterbalance any sins committed. It was almost a book-keeping exercise. Yet the more Luther tried, the more he became convinced that the task was impossible. Humanity was so weighed down with the original sin committed by Adam and Eve that it was hopeless trying to wipe it out. He became deeply depressed about the lack of control he had over his fate. He grew to fear God as a figure of vengeance who punished humanity in eternity for every sin committed in the earthly life.

Luther's sense of despair slowly disappeared with his increasing study of the Bible. He became convinced that here, rather than in the teachings of the Church, lay the true meaning of God's will. In 1516, while locked away in his study, he realised in a flash of inspiration that salvation was secured by what he believed and not by what he did. He no longer saw God as the terrible judge who weighed each life in the balance and rejected those he found wanting, but rather as the God of love who was freely offering salvation to all who would believe in Him and in His son, Jesus Christ. He interpreted the force of the phrase 'by faith are ye saved' as being 'by faith alone are ye saved'. So the Latin phrase *sola fide* (by faith alone) became the central idea of Luther's thinking. Now, for the first time in his life, he felt certain of salvation.

Luther became convinced that the Church's teachings on matters of salvation were fundamentally incorrect. Good works were not only useless in gaining salvation: they could even lead to **damnation** if they were looked upon as a substitute for faith.

Damnation
The state of being condemned to everlasting punishment in hell.

Key term

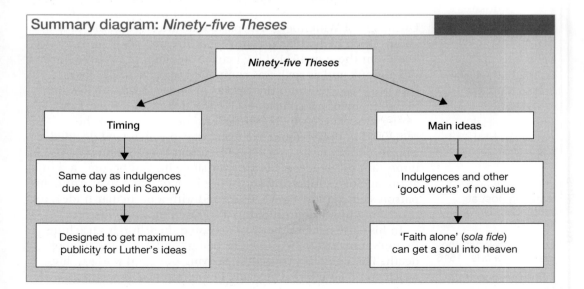

Summary diagram: *Ninety-five Theses*

Ninety-five Theses

Timing

Same day as indulgences due to be sold in Saxony

Designed to get maximum publicity for Luther's ideas

Main ideas

Indulgences and other 'good works' of no value

'Faith alone' (*sola fide*) can get a soul into heaven

3 | Luther's Reasons for Opposing the Church: The Indulgences Controversy

Having made this discovery, Luther's period of personal agony was over. But the implications of the discovery needed to be followed through. This is why the issue of indulgences became so important, because their value, as claimed by Tetzel (see below), depended upon the belief that salvation was to be gained by building up enough merit in God's eyes to counterbalance one's sins. Once it was accepted that 'good works' were a *sign* of being saved rather than the *cause* of it, it was impossible to attach any value to indulgences. This was the stance that Luther took in his *Ninety-five Theses*.

So Luther did not regard disagreements over such matters as the sale of indulgences as merely matters of academic debate. To him it was a question of eternal life and death. He had seen people continue to sin because they felt secure from damnation once they had bought an indulgence which promised them forgiveness for all sins committed during their lifetime, whether past or future. He was convinced that these people were being fatally misled by the Church, and his conscience would not allow him to sit back and do nothing.

Key question
Why did Luther find the indulgences being sold by Tetzel particularly offensive?

Johann Tetzel

The issue had been brought to a head by the activities of Johann Tetzel, a Dominican friar. Tetzel was selling indulgences in the area near to Wittenberg. He was not allowed into the territories of the Elector for fear that he would compete with the indulgences sold in Wittenberg. This was a particularly real fear because Tetzel was selling the most 'powerful' indulgences ever offered. Not only could they assure forgiveness for all the sins of the purchaser, they could even secure the release from purgatory of the soul of a friend or relative who was already dead. In his sermons, which were little more than advertisements encouraging people to buy, Tetzel appealed to his audiences to prove how much they loved their dead parents or children by giving them the most precious gift of all. The jingle ran:

> As soon as the coin in the coffer rings,
> So the soul from purgatory springs.

Tens of thousands of people, including many from Wittenberg who made special journeys to reach Tetzel, invested their savings in indulgences. It was with these events especially in mind that Luther wrote his *Ninety-five Theses*.

Luther hoped that the arguments contained in his theses would convince the Archbishop of Mainz, Albert of Brandenburg, under whose authority Tetzel was operating, that the sale of indulgences should be halted. He therefore sent him a copy of the *Ninety-five Theses*, along with a covering letter in which he explained why he was so concerned.

I do not complain so much of the loud cry of the preacher of indulgences, which I have not heard, but regret the false meaning which the simple folk attach to it, the poor souls believing that when they have purchased such letters they have secured their salvation. Also, that the moment the money jingles in the box souls are delivered from purgatory, and that all sins will be forgiven through a letter of indulgence … And, lastly, that through these indulgences the man is freed from all penalties! Ah, dear God! Thus are those souls which have been committed to your care, dear father, being led in the paths of death, and for them you will be required to render an account.

Johann Tetzel Put to Flight by the Mighty Hero Luther is the title of this pamphlet showing Tetzel going about his business. Why did Luther's *Ninety-five Theses* focus so heavily on the sale of indulgences?

Profile: Johann Tetzel (*c.* 1465–1519)

*c.*1465	– Tetzel was born in Pirna, Saxony, the son of a goldsmith
1482	– Began training for the priesthood at Leipzig University
1488	– Entered the Dominican Order
*c.*1500	– Appointed inquisitor of Leipzig by Cardinal Cajetan
1503	– Authorised by the Pope to sell indulgences within the Holy Roman Empire
1517	– Outraged Luther by selling indulgences on the border of electoral Saxony
1518	– Appointed as a doctor of theology by Frankfurt University
1518	– Retired to a monastery in Leipzig
1519	– Died at Leipzig

Johann Tetzel is significant as the man whose actions shocked Luther into producing the *Ninety-five Theses* – a list of complaints against the Catholic Church which kick-started the Reformation.

Tetzel was a Dominican friar who had been authorised by the Pope to sell 'indulgences' – paper certificates which promised forgiveness of sins. In the past the Catholic Church had clearly insisted that these documents could only have effect if the purchaser was genuinely remorseful for their sins. However, Tetzel brushed aside this subtlety. He entered each town with pomp and ceremony ('God himself could not have been welcomed and received more beautifully,' muttered the reformer Myconius) and then delivered passionate sermons which blackmailed people into parting with their money by asserting that they could save not only their own souls, but also those of dead relatives, from the torments of purgatory:

> Don't you hear the voices of your wailing dead parents and others who say, 'Have mercy upon me, have mercy upon me, because we are in severe punishment and pain. From this you could redeem us with a small alms and yet you do not want to do so.' Open your ears as the father says to the son and the mother to the daughter ... 'We have created you, fed you, cared for you, and left you our temporal goods. Why then are you so cruel and harsh that you do not want to save us, though it only takes a little? You let us lie in flames ...'

After being attacked by Luther, Tetzel defended himself in 1518 with the help of theologians at Frankfurt University but soon found himself isolated and abandoned by the Catholic Church. Tetzel was criticised after the event by prominent theologians such as Cardinal Cajetan, who said that 'Preachers act in the name of the Church so long as they teach the doctrines of Christ and the Church; but if they teach, guided by their own minds and arbitrariness of will, things of which they are ignorant, they cannot pass as representatives of the Church.' Sober Catholics felt that his vulgar extravagances had prejudiced Catholic doctrine, and Miltitz, who was sent from Rome to deal with the situation, told him off severely. He hid himself in the Dominican convent at Leipzig in fear of popular violence, and died there on 4 July 1519, just as Luther was beginning his famous disputation with Johann Eck.

Although the theology preached by Tetzel has been condemned by both Protestants and Catholics alike, there is disagreement about his moral character. Luther, with his taste for personal abuse, hinted that Tetzel had committed adultery in Ratisbon and had escaped imprisonment only due to the intervention of the Elector of Saxony. Tetzel was also accused of embezzling funds, but again there is no hard evidence of this. Money could only be deposited into a coffer which had two or three locks and could only be opened in the presence of a notary. We know that Luther was fond of a good story: another favourite of his was that Tetzel had been asked by a German nobleman whether indulgences could assure forgiveness for sins not yet committed; when Tetzel eagerly replied in the affirmative, the nobleman handed over his money and then beat up Tetzel, claiming that this was the sin he had planned all along.

Albert of Brandenburg

The Archbishop of Mainz, Albert of Brandenburg, was disturbed by this potential threat to his plans. He was relying on the money raised from the sale of indulgences to pay off the debts he had incurred in securing the agreement of the Pope to his acquisition of the archbishopric (although it was popularly believed that the money was to finance the rebuilding of St Peter's Cathedral in Rome). Albert was still in his early twenties and had had no religious training, but he had already bought his way into a bishopric and two archbishoprics, each of which carried with it large territories over which he was the sole ruler. In the process he had become one of the most powerful princes in Germany.

Key question
Why did Albert of Brandenburg feel so threatened by Luther's protest?

4 | The Spread of the *Ninety-five Theses*

Albert felt greatly threatened by Luther, whose *Ninety-five Theses* were rapidly translated into German, printed and widely distributed. Many people agreed with Luther's comments. Those who understood **theology** recognised the strength of Luther's attack on indulgences, while others shared his resentment at the way in which the poor of Germany were constantly pressurised into paying money to the Church, much of which went to a foreigner – the Pope in Rome. Luther's appeal to the sentiments of ordinary Germans was clear:

Theology
The study of religion, in particular the relationship between God and humanity. Its students are known as theologians.

Key term

> Christians should be taught that, unless they abound in possessions beyond their needs, their duty is to retain what is necessary for their own household, and in no way to squander it in buying indulgences … Christians should be taught that, if the Pope knew the exactions of the preachers of indulgences, he would rather have St Peter's Church in Rome reduced to ashes than built with the skin, flesh and bones of his sheep.

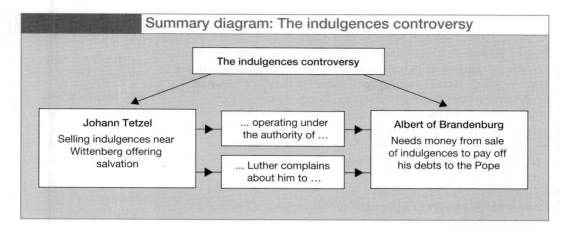

Summary diagram: The indulgences controversy

The indulgences controversy

Johann Tetzel
Selling indulgences near Wittenberg offering salvation

... operating under the authority of ...

... Luther complains about him to ...

Albert of Brandenburg
Needs money from sale of indulgences to pay off his debts to the Pope

5 | Attempts to Silence Luther, 1517–21

Luther is threatened by Cardinal Cajetan

Key questions
What steps were taken to silence Luther between 1518 and 1520? Why were they unsuccessful? Why did the initial attempts to silence Luther fail so dismally?

Albert immediately appealed to the Pope for support, requesting that Luther be silenced. Given the great distances over which correspondence had to travel, the reaction of the Pope, Leo X (1513–21), was swift. Luther was ordered to come to Rome. He refused. So Cardinal Cajetan was sent to Germany to deal with him. Cajetan summoned Luther to meet him in Augsburg in October 1518 and made it clear that the Pope's patience was running out. For several days, Cajetan bullied Luther by threatening terrible punishments if he did not withdraw his criticisms of the Church.

Key date

Luther was summoned to Augsburg and threatened by Cardinal Cajetan: 1518

Luther remained unmoved. His position had been clearly stated from the outset, and his conscience would not allow him to change it. He argued that he had identified mistakes in the Church's teachings. He could abandon his point of view only if he could either be shown evidence from the Bible which proved him wrong, or be convinced of his errors by 'sound reason'. The Church's position was equally clear. It maintained that it was for the Pope alone to interpret the Bible and to decide the teaching of the Church. The duty of all Catholics was to obey him as God's representative on earth. The Church therefore had no need to convince anybody of anything. It merely had to insist on good discipline. Thus the two sides were arguing at cross purposes with no real point of contact.

Luther is questioned by Johann Eck

Key question
In what ways did the debate with Eck push Luther into a more radical position?

After Cajetan's unsuccessful mission the Pope realised that threats against Luther were never going to work. The Church was offering no defence to Luther's charges and was leaving the way clear for him to gain increasing numbers of supporters in Germany. The Pope was so unpopular in Germany due to his extortionate taxes that the traditional appeal to unthinking obedience was being rejected. So it was decided to meet Luther's challenge in open debate.

The Catholics win a technical victory

A formal debate was arranged to take place in Leipzig in July 1519. Doctor Johann Eck was chosen to uphold the Church's position. He was recognised as being the most skilful debater in Germany. For 18 days the issues were argued before a panel of 'neutral' academics, in the presence of local officials. Eck won the competition in technical terms. He scored numerous debating points, trapping Luther into putting forward some indefensible arguments. But Luther's passion and conviction impressed observers more than Eck's cold logic.

Luther clarifies his position

Luther had come to Leipzig with the reputation of being a tiresome rebel who just needed to be brought under control. However, the debate gave him the reputation of an inspirational revolutionary. Eck was responsible for the change. This is because he forced Luther to take each of his arguments to its logical conclusion. In particular, Eck agreed with Luther that the Bible provided no evidence that indulgences could guarantee salvation. However, Eck pointed out that neither was there any mention of purgatory, or of several sacraments, or even of a Pope – yet surely Luther did not deny the authority of these things as well? To Eck's astonishment, Luther did indeed reject all of these things too. Luther had already developed the idea that entry into heaven could only be through *sola fide* (faith alone). Now, he developed his second revolutionary idea: that the way of searching for that faith was through *sola scriptura* (scripture alone).

Luther had started off by merely claiming that the Pope was exceeding his powers. Suddenly, he was claiming that the Pope had no special powers at all! Instead of merely seeking the reform of **abuses**, Luther was now challenging the very foundations of the Church itself. Early in the disputation Eck had accused Luther of following the ideas of the heretic Jan Huss, who had been burned for challenging the authority of the Pope a century before (for more on Huss, see Chapter 3). This failed to discredit Luther in the eyes of the German princes. Neither did it frighten Luther. By the end of the debate Luther was proud to admit that he agreed with the main ideas of his Czech predecessor who had been declared a heretic and burned for his beliefs.

Luther is excommunicated by Pope Leo X

Following the Leipzig debate, Pope Leo X decided that Luther should suffer **excommunication**. This would be done by sending him a legal document, a **bull** informing him that he was an outcast from the Church. This meant not only that all obedient Christians would refuse to have any dealings with him, but also that his soul would be condemned to burn in hell forever. To ensure that this was known, the bull would be read from the pulpit of every church. The Bull of Excommunication, known by

Key terms

Abuses
Instances of corruption in the Church.

Excommunication
The act of casting someone out of the Church, resulting in their being destined for hell.

Bull
A document containing orders given directly by the Pope in Rome.

Key dates

Luther developed the idea of *sola scriptura*: 1519

Luther was excommunicated by Pope Leo X: 1520

Key question
What was the significance of the papal bull, *Exsurge Domine*?

its first words, *Exsurge Domine* ('Lord, cast out'), was issued in June 1520. Luther showed his contempt for the Pope by burning the Bull publicly. Shortly afterwards, he produced a vicious pamphlet whose title *Against the Bull of the Antichrist* claimed that the Pope was the devil! This was the point of no return for Luther.

Luther is outlawed by Emperor Charles V

Key question
To what extent was the Diet of Worms a victory for the Pope?

At this point, the Pope called upon Emperor Charles V to bring Luther under control. The Pope's strategy was a sensible one. Firstly, Frederick of Saxony owed obedience to the Holy Roman Emperor, as did all the rulers of the states in Germany. Secondly, Emperor Charles V was a strong Catholic who was determined to uphold the interests of the Church.

Charles invites Luther to attend the Diet of Worms

Key question
Why did Charles V give Luther the chance to speak at the Diet of Worms?

Charles had become emperor in 1519 while still a teenager. By then, he was already the King of Spain and the Duke of Burgundy (an area based around the Netherlands of today). He was potentially one of the most powerful European monarchs in history. He arrived in Germany in time for a Diet that was to take place in the city of Worms in April 1521. The Church authorities hoped that the Diet would condemn Luther without even giving him a hearing. They argued that his publications were by now so numerous and so clearly heretical that no defence was possible. But Charles decided to allow Luther to make an appearance so that there could be no complaint of unfair treatment. Luther was summoned to appear at Worms under a promise of '**safe conduct**' which would protect him from arrest whatever the outcome of his hearing.

Key term

Safe conduct
A promise that no harm will come to someone if they agree to travel to meet someone.

Luther attends against the advice of his friends

Key question
Why did Luther's friends advise him not to attend the Diet of Worms?

Luther's closest associates advised him not to appear. It was well known that, according to the Church's teaching, there was no need to keep one's promises to a heretic. It was also remembered that Jan Huss had been arrested and executed while under a promise of safe conduct. But Luther wasn't too concerned about his chances of survival. He regarded himself as being in God's hands, and was sure that if God meant him to live he would return safely from Worms. One thing he was certain of was that God wished him to preach the truth as widely as possible. So he travelled to Worms.

Luther defends his position

Key question
Why did Luther refuse to retract his writings?

Even now the Pope's representatives hoped to limit Luther's participation to answering two questions:

- whether the books and pamphlets that had appeared in his name were really his, and
- whether he was prepared to abandon the views contained in them.

Luther asked to be allowed to consider the questions overnight. His request was granted. On the next morning he answered 'Yes' to the first question, but said that it was impossible to give a one-word answer to the second question. He then proceeded to explain this point in a way which allowed him another opportunity to advertise his main ideas.

Firstly, he said, some of his writings agreed with the teachings of the Church, so it made no sense for him to reject these.

Secondly, he had produced writings against the papacy, but he stood by these because they attacked:

> Men who both by their beliefs as well as the disgraceful example of their lives have utterly laid waste the Christian world with evil both of the spirit and the flesh. This fact none can deny or conceal. The experience of everybody and the complaints of the whole world bear witness that through the laws of the Pope … the consciences of Christians have been most horribly entrapped … Further, property and possessions, especially in this illustrious land of Germany, have been devoured by an unbelievable **tyranny** … If I retract these writings, it would be … supplying strength to this tyranny.

Thirdly, Luther refused to retract the comments he had made against the supporters of the papacy:

> There is a third kind of book which I have written against certain private, and as they call them, distinguished individuals. These are they who endeavour to maintain the Roman tyranny and to destroy the holiness taught by me. Against these I confess I have been more severe than befits my religion or my profession. But then I do not set myself up as a saint. It is not my life I am arguing about, but the teaching of Christ. It is not right for me to retract these works, because this very retraction would again bring about a state of affairs where tyranny and ungodliness would rule and rage among the people of God more violently than they ever ruled before.

Luther concluded his speech by challenging his opponents to prove that anything he said was against the word of God:

> [I invite] your most serene Majesty, most illustrious lordships, or any one at all, whether of high or low estate [to] expose my errors, overthrow me by the writings of the prophets and evangelists. I am more than ready, if the case be proven, to retract every error no matter what it is. I shall be the first to consign my books to the flames.

The Church authorities reply

Equally clear was the Church's case against Luther, which had remained constant throughout and had become stronger as he provided more and more evidence of his heretical thinking.

> Is it not the case that you want Holy Scripture to be understood by your whim and your ideas? … Is it right to open to question and drag into dispute, those matters which the Catholic Church has carefully settled, matters which have turned upon [beliefs] which our fathers held with absolute faith … indeed they would rather have endured a

Key term

Tyranny
An evil dictatorship. The person in charge of such a regime is described as a *tyrant*.

Key question
How did the Church authorities respond to Luther's criticisms at Worms?

thousand deaths than have departed from them a hair's breadth? ... Do not, I beg you, Martin [claim] that you are the one and only person ... who alone grasps the true sense of Holy Scripture ... Do not make your judgement superior to that of so many of the most brilliant men. Do not seem to be wiser than all others.

It was, of course, the political implications of Luther's position that were uppermost in the minds of many of his opponents.

He despises the authority of the Church Fathers, an authority the Church accepts. He utterly takes away obedience and authority, and writes nothing which does not have the effect of promoting ... war, murder, robbery [and] the complete collapse of the Christian faith. He teaches a loose, self-willed kind of life, without any kind of law, utterly brutish ... As he shows as much regard for the secular sword as he does for the Pope's excommunication and its penalties, so has he done greater harm to secular law and order.

Key question
How and why did Charles V refuse to compromise with Luther?

Charles V delivers his verdict in the Edict of Worms

Given the evidence, there could be only one outcome of Luther's trial at Worms – he was found guilty of heresy. However, Luther's supporters hoped that the Emperor would at least compromise by restricting the power of the Church in Germany. They were bitterly disappointed. In the Edict of Worms Charles announced that Luther and all who supported him would be punished unless they immediately agreed to accept the teachings and authority of the Church. The terms of the bull *Exsurge Domine* should be carried out – citizens of the Empire had to burn Luther's writings wherever they were found and refuse to provide Luther or his supporters with food or shelter. Anyone failing to do these things would be imprisoned and lose all their property. The Pope had got everything he wanted – except Luther's imprisonment.

Key date
Luther was outlawed by Emperor Charles V at the Diet of Worms: April 1521

Martin Luther as a monk, by Lucas Cranach, 1520. Is the artist of this illustration sympathetic or hostile to Luther?

Luther is protected by Frederick the Wise

Luther was not the first theologian in western Europe to take up this revolutionary position. But he was the first who was able both to maintain it and to avoid being put to death as a heretic. Others before him had either retracted their criticisms or had been killed. Why did this not happen to Luther?

Key question
What was the significance of Frederick's decision to protect Luther?

Luther is kidnapped by his own supporters

One reason why Luther survived is that in May 1521, even before the Edict of Worms was announced, he left the city. He had been persuaded by powerful supporters that there was nothing to be gained by remaining and much to be lost if some Catholic enthusiast decided to take the law into his own hands. His 'escape' from Worms was well planned, as was his subsequent disappearance. As he and his escort were passing through a forest on their way to Wittenberg, they were seized by a group of unidentified horsemen who then rode off with Luther as their 'captive'.

The man responsible for Luther's 'kidnap' was none other than his staunchest supporter, **Elector** Frederick 'the Wise' of Saxony (see below). Frederick had decided that the political situation was too uncertain for the 'notorious heretic' to be anywhere but in hiding. Luther was taken to Frederick's castle at Wartburg, where he disguised himself by growing a beard and adopting the name of 'Farmer George' before starting work on a German translation of the Bible.

Key question
How did Frederick the Wise protect Luther?

Luther was 'kidnapped' and hidden by Frederick the Wise at Wartburg Castle: May 1521

Elector
One of the seven princes who elected the Holy Roman Emperor.

Frederick's power and authority

A second reason for Luther's survival is that he lived in the German state of electoral Saxony where the Pope's direct influence was minimal. Frederick the Wise was one of the seven electors of the Empire. This meant he was a member of an elite group of territorial rulers whose influence was considerable. The Emperor required their agreement before he could take action of any significance, and he was careful not to upset them without very good reason. Frederick the Wise was sympathetic to Luther from the start, and Leo X, who wished to retain Frederick's support within Germany, was unwilling to risk angering him. He preferred to wait until Luther had been given every opportunity to recant. If persuasion failed he could then call upon Frederick to do his duty as a Christian prince; hence the efforts made to persuade Luther that he was wrong to challenge the authority of the Church. However, Frederick was not prepared to be manipulated by Pope Leo.

Frederick was not only powerful but also highly esteemed. His nickname 'the Wise' seems to have been justified. He was generally regarded as the outstanding ruler in Germany, and as a man whose judgement was to be respected. When, before the election of Charles V, there had been behind-the-scenes scheming to break the hold of the Habsburgs on the imperial title, it had been Frederick's name that had been put forward as the one likely to command general support.

Key question
Why was Frederick able to defy the Pope and Emperor Charles V?

Key date

Key term

Frederick III, the Wise, Elector of Saxony, (1463–1525)

1463		– Frederick was born
1486		– Succeeded his father as Elector of Saxony
1502		– Founded the University of Wittenberg
1511		– Employs Luther as a lecturer at the University of Wittenberg
1518		– Offers protection to Luther following the threats of Cardinal Cajetan
1519		– Voted for Charles V to become the Holy Roman Emperor
1520		– Refused to carry out the papal bull ordering that Luther's writings should be burned
1521	May	– Hid Luther at Wartburg Castle following the Edict of Worms
1525		– Died unmarried and childless. His younger brother John – a dedicated Lutheran – succeeded him as Elector of Saxony

Frederick of Saxony is significant as the most powerful early defender of Martin Luther. Frederick 'the Wise' was a cultured and educated man who was much respected for his sense of justice. He was a great diplomat who managed to keep Saxony out of all wars while he was its elector. He founded the University of Wittenberg in 1502 and encouraged the brightest intellectuals to work there. Luther was sent there to serve as a lecturer by his Augustinian order in 1511 and Frederick quickly came to appreciate his talents.

Following the death of the Holy Roman Emperor in 1519, Frederick was the Pope's favoured candidate to take over the job. However, Frederick refused to stand for the post and also refused to be bribed into supporting either of the two main candidates for the position – King Francis I of France and Charles I of Spain. Instead, he reached an independent decision to cast his vote for Charles, who duly became the new Holy Roman Emperor.

Despite the threats of Cardinal Cajetan at Augsburg in 1518, Luther refused to withdraw his criticisms of the Church and instead considered going into exile. However, Frederick offered to protect Luther from his enemies. The papal bull which excommunicated Luther and ordered his writings to be burned was never carried out in Saxony. It was also Frederick who persuaded Charles V that Luther should be allowed to defend himself at the Diet of Worms. When the Emperor outlawed Luther in the Edict of Worms, Frederick 'kidnapped' Luther for his own protection and hid him away at Wartburg Castle. Frederick then negotiated with the Emperor to ensure that the Edict of Worms did not have to be enforced within Saxony.

Despite these actions, Frederick never formally converted to Lutheranism. He amassed a personal collection of over 19,000 holy relics during his lifetime – which of course Luther regarded as pointless – and died a Catholic in 1525. He also had very little personal contact with Luther, since he realised that the Church could use a close relationship between the two men as evidence that Frederick had been 'bewitched' by the heretic. Instead, Frederick kept Luther at a distance and refused to make direct comments about his case, even at the Diet of Worms.

Why, then, did Frederick protect Luther at all? There are a number of possible reasons. The indulgence-seller Johann Tetzel was working for Frederick's rival, Albert of Mainz. Luther's attack on the 'foreign' Pope's exploitation of Germany appealed to Frederick's sense of nationalism. The way the Church condemned Luther as a heretic without using evidence from the Bible was an affront to Frederick's sense of justice. Frederick was not keen that the reputation of his new university and the quality of its lecturers should be damaged by accusations of heresy by the Church. Finally, Frederick was sensitive to the religious beliefs of his younger brother John 'the Steadfast' who was a committed Lutheran.

Frederick's motivation

It is widely accepted that without Frederick's protection Luther would have been executed as a heretic early in his career as a reformer. Yet it is not fully clear why the Elector acted as he did, eventually risking the anger of all who had the right and the power to act against him. It was not that he came under the personal influence of Luther. He was careful to keep a distance between them so that he could always claim that he had not met the man whom he was defending. In this way it was impossible for his opponents to claim that he had been bewitched. His motivations can be summarised as follows:

Key question
Why was Frederick so determined to support Luther?

- Political: At first Frederick's motivation seems to have been purely political. Luther's attacks on Tetzel were, in effect, attacks on Albert of Brandenburg. The rivalry between Albert's and Frederick's families for influence in Germany was intense, so it was only natural that Frederick should defend a subject who was attacking his enemy.
- Nationalistic: Frederick was also motivated by German nationalism. For many years there had been widespread resentment in Germany that the papacy had been able to extract huge quantities of money from the country in a way that was not possible in Spain, France or England (this theme is dealt with in more detail in Chapter 3). Luther tapped this reservoir of anti-papal feeling and appealed to a common hatred of the grasping foreigner. Frederick shared these sentiments. When Luther was summoned to Rome by Pope Leo he was able to refuse because Frederick was firmly behind him and was arguing that any case against Luther should be heard on German soil. Even when the

bull *Exsurge Domine* was issued against Luther, Frederick refused to obey it. He claimed that it carried no weight until Luther had been given an opportunity to answer the charges against him in person and in Germany.

- Religious: Yet there was more to Frederick's support of Luther than these 'political' issues. Although he was not an early convert to the new religious beliefs, his brother John 'the Steadfast' was a committed Lutheran, and Frederick was sensitive to this. Frederick was also sufficiently interested and in touch with what Luther was teaching to understand that something of major importance was taking place in his small capital city. He was not prepared to stop it or to allow others to stop it until the rightness or otherwise of Luther's claims had been fairly decided. This meant approaching the issue with an open mind, which the Church was clearly failing to do.

In his dealings with the problem of what to do about Luther, Frederick seems to have started by acting in what he saw as his own best interests. Within a short time, however, it appears that his determination to see 'fair play' and his developing feeling that Luther was probably right took over as the main motivating forces that led him to make certain that Luther remained safe despite the storm that was gathering against him.

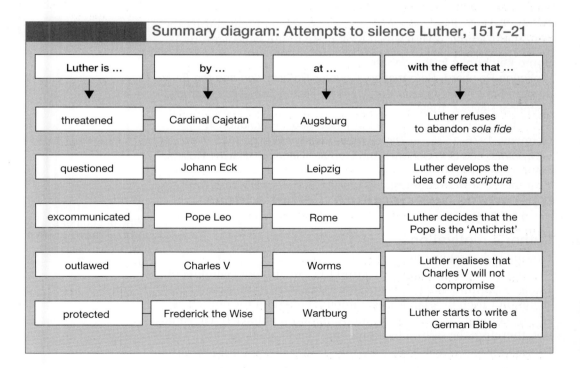

Luther is ...	by ...	at ...	with the effect that ...
threatened	Cardinal Cajetan	Augsburg	Luther refuses to abandon *sola fide*
questioned	Johann Eck	Leipzig	Luther develops the idea of *sola scriptura*
excommunicated	Pope Leo	Rome	Luther decides that the Pope is the 'Antichrist'
outlawed	Charles V	Worms	Luther realises that Charles V will not compromise
protected	Frederick the Wise	Wartburg	Luther starts to write a German Bible

Summary diagram: Attempts to silence Luther, 1517–21

The key debate

Historians continue to debate the question:

Was the Reformation a German Nationalist movement?

The great nineteenth-century German historian, Leopold von Ranke, established the Lutheran Reformation as a decisive step towards the creation of the German nation state which eventually became a political reality in 1871. In his view, the Reformation was a struggle by the German people to cast off the control of a corrupt foreign power – the papacy – and to pursue their own purified version of Christianity.

Ranke's view has since been developed and challenged in a number of respects. For example, the Marxist historian Max Steinmetz shared Ranke's view that the Reformation was a German national revolution; however, he argued that this revolution was not a religious revolution led by the ruling elites, but was instead a social revolution led by the peasant masses. It was, in his words, 'The first attempt of the popular masses to create a unified national state from below.'

Another challenge to the Rankean idea has been provided by Schilling and Reinhard (historians already mentioned in the key debate in Chapter 1). They agree with Ranke that the Reformation was crucial in forming national identities, but disagree that this development was limited to Germany. The cultural identity of England was very sharply defined by its Reformation under the Tudor monarchs, as has been demonstrated by historians such as Diarmaid MacCulloch; so too was that of Spain and Italy during the period of Catholic revival which took place in the same century.

Some key books in the debate:

Wolfgang Reinhard, *Reformation, Counter-Reformation and the Early Modern State: A Reassessment*, Catholic Historical Review (Catholic Historical Review, 1989)

Max Steinmetz, 'Theses on the Early Bourgeois Revolution in Germany, 1476–1535', in *The German Peasant War of 1525: New Viewpoints*, eds Bob Scribner and Gerhard Benecke (Harper Collins, 1979)

6 | Towards *Sola Scriptura*: Luther's Ideas 1517–21

Key question
Why did Luther's protest develop into a full-blown crisis for the Church?

Luther's motivation

How had what seemed to start as a minor disagreement grown to such proportions? Much of the answer lies in an understanding of Luther's motivation. He was not interested in acquiring power or riches, nor even in establishing a public reputation for himself as an outstanding theologian. He was in no way a politician. He could not, therefore, be swayed by arguments that focused on the consequences of his actions – on what others might think, say or do as a result of the stand he was taking. He did not really mind whether he lived or died. He did not care about the factors that influence most people's actions, such as the desires to be happy, rich, famous, loved, approved of, successful – or merely to survive.

Luther's interests were selfish but were truly other-worldly. His overriding concern was with his own salvation. In common with many people of his own and earlier ages, he recognised that one's earthly life was likely to be painful and short. Sickness and death were commonplace and constantly gave reminders of the temporary nature of the body and other material things. What mattered was the soul. It had the potential for eternal life, against which the few years spent on earth were insignificant.

The idea of *sola fide*

Key question
Why was the attack on indulgences so controversial?

Thus what may have appeared to be a disagreement over a minor, and relatively recent, practice of the Church – the sale of indulgences – was actually the result of differences on matters of fundamental importance. On the one hand, there was no possibility that Luther, given his total personal commitment to the idea of *sola fide*, would be prepared to compromise. On the other hand, the Catholic Church was equally committed to the idea of good works as a method of salvation. So a collision course was unavoidable from the very start.

The idea of *sola scriptura*

Key question
What were the implications of Luther becoming an evangelical?

What made the conflict between Luther and the papacy so much more than a theological dispute was the way in which Luther thought through the implications of his ideas in the three years between the *Ninety-five Theses* and the bull *Exsurge Domine*. In the process he became a complete evangelical, in that the only authority he would accept for a religious belief or practice was the Bible. This led him to reject the Pope's claim of being God's appointed representative on earth, entrusted with the keys of heaven, because no justification for this could be found in the Bible. So for Luther the whole structure of authority within the Church was invalid. This meant that neither the Pope nor anybody under his control had any right to pass judgement on Luther's ideas. It was for this reason that, when the bull *Exsurge Domine* was burned publicly, the books of **canon law**, which defined the legal powers and practices of the Church, were also thrown into the flames. Luther was rejecting any authority that could not be justified by the Bible.

Key term

Canon law
Laws to do with the governance of the Church.

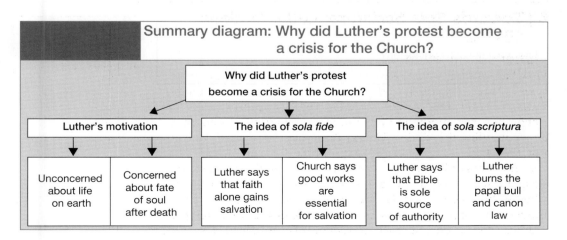

Summary diagram: Why did Luther's protest become a crisis for the Church?

Why did Luther's protest become a crisis for the Church?		
Luther's motivation	**The idea of *sola fide***	**The idea of *sola scriptura***
Unconcerned about life on earth / Concerned about fate of soul after death	Luther says that faith alone gains salvation / Church says good works are essential for salvation	Luther says that Bible is sole source of authority / Luther burns the papal bull and canon law

Study Guide: AS Questions

In the style of Edexcel

How important was the support of Frederick the Wise to the survival of Lutheranism in the period to 1521?   (30 marks)

Exam tips

The cross-references are intended to take you straight to the material that will help you to answer the question.

This question is essentially asking you why Lutheranism survived, but, in answering a question of this type, where one reason is given to you in the question, you should plan to give substantial attention to this factor – probably about one-third of your answer – and you should make sure you deal with the factor in your conclusion, even if you are going to conclude that other factors are more important.

When you plan, keep the focus on the question. It's not asking you why a Lutheran movement developed, or why Lutheranism spread. You would use much of the same material, but it needs to be shaped to fit the demands of the question. Here you need first to think about what might have prevented Lutheranism from surviving, and then you can decide whether Frederick's support was crucial or just helpful. Your answer will then be focused on how important his support was. Do also be careful to note the time frame of the question – you are not asked to go beyond 1521.

Below is a list of factors to include in your response. In what order will you use them? What information will you select to develop them?

- Challenges to Luther and Lutheranism (see pages 29, 31, 32).
- The position and influence of Frederick the Wise (see pages 34–37).
- The nature of the support and protection Frederick gave to Luther (see pages 34–37).
- Luther's role (see pages 25, 31, 38).
- Support for Luther's teaching and criticism of the Catholic Church (see pages 25–28).

And what is your conclusion?

In the style of OCR A

Study the five sources on the impact of Luther's *Ninety-five Theses*, and then answer **both** sub-questions. It is recommended that you spend two-thirds of your time in answering part **(b)**.

(a) Study Sources B and C.
Compare these sources as evidence for the reactions of the papacy towards Luther's teaching. (30 marks)

(b) Study all the sources.
Use your own knowledge to assess how far the sources support the interpretation that the publication of the *Ninety-five Theses* in 1517 did not represent a serious challenge to the Church.
(70 marks)
(Total: 100 marks)

The Impact of Luther's *Ninety-five Theses*
Source A
Luther, letter to Christopher Scheurl, early in 1518
Luther claims in a letter to a religious teacher sympathetic to Luther's cause that the impact of the *Ninety-five Theses* was not intended:

I did not wish to have my Theses circulated widely. I only intended submitting them to a few learned men for examination, and if they disapproved, to suppress them. But now they are being spread abroad and translated everywhere, which I never would have believed, so that I regret writing them. This is not because I am unwilling to tell the truth but because this way of instructing the people is unwise. I am still uncertain about some points, would have gone into others in more detail and would have left out others completely if I had predicted all this.

Source B
Pope Leo X, letter to Duke George of Saxony, October 1518
The Pope strongly condemns Luther's writings:

Martin Luther, at the suggestion of the Devil, has said evil about us and the papacy, in preaching and cursing. This resembles heresy and deserves severe punishment. Because of your devotion and obedience to the papacy, it should not be tolerated. We should root up this weed from God's field in case it takes root among simple people.

Source C
Luther's publication, Proceedings at Augsburg, *November 1518*
An account by Luther of his debate in October 1518 with Cardinal Cajetan, the Pope's representative in Germany:

Cajetan stated that he did not wish to argue with me, but to settle the matter peacefully and in a fatherly fashion. He said that the Pope demanded that I should do three things. First, I should come to my senses and withdraw my errors, secondly promise not to repeat them in the future, and thirdly I should not do anything to disturb the Church. I immediately asked to be told how I had been wrong because I was not conscious of any errors. I declared that I was not conscious of having said anything contrary to the Bible, the Church Fathers or papal announcements. All that I said seems to me entirely sensible, true and Catholic. Nevertheless, since I am a man who can make a mistake, I would submit to the judgement of the Church and to all who were better informed than me.

Source D
Duke George of Saxony, letter to the Chancellor of Leipzig University, January 1519
An important German prince calls for a debate about Luther's writings:

The University has always been a place for all kinds of learning, where anybody could debate or propose whatever he liked, as long as it was within the Catholic faith. Leipzig University has had many debates on the Mass and other religious matters. No one has been prevented from speaking. We think that a debate ought to be held about whether or not a soul springs to heaven as soon as a penny rings in the indulgence plate. It seems good to have a decision on the matter to stop poor, ignorant people from being deceived.

Source E
A. Johnston, The Protestant Reformation in Europe, *1992*
A modern historian comments on developments in 1518:

There is little doubt that if Leo X had immediately corrected the worst abuses surrounding indulgences, the affair could have been settled quickly. However, such clarification was not forthcoming until November 1518. Albert of Brandenburg had forwarded his copy of the *Ninety-five Theses* to Rome as early as February 1518, but the Pope was slow to act. Leo took up the matter with Gabriel Venetus, the head of the Augustinian order, and the request to silence Luther was then passed on to Staupitz. However, when the Augustinians failed to deal with the issue at the meeting of their order at Heidelberg in 1518, at which Luther was present, the Dominicans took up the cause. The Dominicans were the natural rivals and enemies of the Augustinians and they leapt to Tetzel's defence. One of their number, Sylvester Prierias, drafted a reply to Luther and it was he who shifted the focus from indulgences to papal authority.

Exam tips

(a) In a comparison of two sources, you must make direct references to the sources themselves, identify any similarities and differences, and comment on the nature of the sources' authenticity, completeness, consistency, typicality and usefulness. You are not expected to consider all of these qualities but to discuss the most important. Remember that you should only use your own knowledge to provide a context for the sources and your answer should not be driven by contextual knowledge. Some of the main points you might discuss are:

- Both sources express concern at Luther's ideas but while Source B fears ordinary people might misinterpret them, Source C wants to be sure the ideas are correct.
- The papacy in Source B privately condemns Luther as a heretic but in Source C is publicly willing to allow a theological debate to take place.
- The papacy in Source B expects Duke George, a staunch Catholic and patron of Leipzig University, to put pressure on his cousin, Frederick the Wise, who was patron of Luther's University of Wittenberg. This suggests that the Pope was not confident that Cajetan or other papal agents would be able to silence Luther and a more political approach was needed.
- Luther claims that the papacy wished to settle the argument peacefully but Leo privately assumed a more belligerent attitude. As the letter (Source B) was not intended for publication, the Pope was expressing his genuine concerns; Luther's statement (Source C) was for general consumption and may reflect his desire to appear cooperative and reasonable. In fact neither man had any intention of changing his mind.

(b) The answer requires a good balance between your own knowledge and an analysis of all five sources. Your answer might consider some of the following points:

- Luther in Source A was concerned that he might be misunderstood due to the premature publication of his *Theses*, a view confirmed in Sources B and D, but in Luther's opinion, due to any theological inaccuracies rather than popular misunderstandings.
- Luther's *Theses* only attacked Church abuses but as Source E points out, the attack was taken by the Church to be a challenge on the integrity and authority of the papacy itself.

- Luther claims in Source C that all he wanted was to debate his views publicly, a view shared by Duke George in Source D but the Dominicans in Source E raised issues concerning papal authority, which Luther might have considered but in 1518 had not yet formulated.
- Most sources support the interpretation that the *Ninety-five Theses* did not present a serious challenge but Source B implies the papacy's private concerns, Source D shares some concerns that ignorant people may be deceived, and so asks for a debate, and Source E states that the papacy allowed the affair to get out of control and so become a threat to the Church.

In the style of OCR B

Answer **both** parts of your chosen question.

(a) How is the writing of the *Ninety-five Theses* best explained?
[Explaining actions]   (25 marks)

(b) What was it about Luther that made him such a threat that he was excommunicated in 1521?
[Explaining ideas, attitudes, beliefs and circumstances]
                                                          (25 marks)

Exam tips

General introduction

In this exam paper you always have two pairs of questions and you have to answer both parts of one pair. In your chosen pair, each question will be different so each needs full and separate treatment. Each question in your pair is equally weighted so spend equal time on part **(a)** and part **(b)**. Both must be answered with an essay.

All questions in this exam paper require an answer that explains and makes sense of the past. Your task is to construct that historical explanation. The information in the square bracket below each question identifies for you the kind of explanation that you need to start off working with. To prepare a good answer for each essay, you have to work through four stages: (i) identify the various factors that explain the question set. There will always be more than one and they will be a mixture of ideas, actions and events; (ii) work out the role that each factor played; (iii) decide which factor or factors were more important than the others so that you can explain why, and back up your claims with supporting evidence; (iv) establish why and how some of those factors influenced others, again, with supporting evidence so you can justify your arguments.

Work through each of those four steps in rough and you have got your essay plan. Write up each stage and you have got your essay – well structured and focused on the question. If you only complete step (i), your answer will be just a basic list of ideas, actions and events so it will not score well. If you complete steps (ii) and (iii), your answer will have arranged those ideas, actions and events according to their relative importance. That explanation of the issue set will be quite advanced so it will score in Level 4 (16 to 20 marks) *if* you really have explained things carefully. To reach the top level (21 to 25 marks), you have to go one stage further and simultaneously explain the interaction of component ideas, actions and events – not just putting them in rank order of importance but establishing cause and effect from one to another. Do all of that and you will have given an excellent answer and constructed a strong historical explanation that makes real sense of the past and shows that you don't merely know what happened but understand what was going on, and why. The guidance in each of the chapters isn't built around the only possible answer to each question – there is never only one answer in History. They are examples to show you *how* to construct a successful historical explanation.

(a) Note the limits of the question: don't rush off into a general survey of the causes of the Reformation.

Firstly, make notes on the short-term events: Luther's concerns with Tetzel's sale of indulgences in 1517. Secondly, make notes explaining the mid-term developments: examine 1517 in the context of Luther's developing thought during the 1510s – were Tetzel and that indulgence all there was to it or was Luther so volatile by 1517 that events in Saxony in July–October 1517 were only the spark? Thirdly, you need to move beyond Luther the individual towards more deep-seated factors. Consider any relationship between Luther's troubles and the state of the late medieval church (see Chapter 3): go back to the *Theses* themselves and establish to what extent those general grievances show up in what Luther wrote about. Finally, pull things together in a conclusion, but don't make the mistake of deciding that the answer is a simple 'either/or'. Luther was not operating in a vacuum, but neither was he just being carried along by the fashionable ideas of the moment.

(b) The prompt here suggests you start to consider ideas and beliefs – not a straight comparison of the differences between Luther and Rome, but an explanation focused on differences that threatened Catholicism in general and Rome in particular. That means issues of authority, e.g. the authority of the Catholic Clergy and its sacraments challenged by Luther's doctrine of *sola fide* and *sola scriptura*, culminating in the excommunication of

Luther by the Pope. However, you should then move away from narrowly theological explanations towards a broader interpretation: the political, nationalistic and religious dimension that lay behind both Emperor Charles V's decision to declare Luther an outlaw of the Empire and also Frederick of Saxony's decision to protect him. In other words, you need to show how and why Luther's teachings threatened not just religious beliefs but the social and political roles of the Pope and the Holy Roman Emperor.

3 Causes of the Reformation

POINTS TO CONSIDER

The arguments between Lutherans and Catholics centred on issues of religious belief and practice. So to explain why the Reformation occurred, some historians start by considering what was so appealing about Luther's religious ideas. However, the cause of a major historical event like the Reformation can never be explained in terms of just one factor. As a result, other historians regard the Reformation primarily as a social revolution against a Church which was considered meddlesome, grasping and restrictive. Still others argue that the most important factor was political – the German princes wanted to restrict the power of foreigners in their territories. It is also possible to explain the Reformation in terms of cultural factors. The Renaissance rejected blind obedience to authority and instead focused on the judgement and potential within every human being; Martin Luther simply used these principles to question the beliefs and practices of the Catholic Church, with dramatic results.

This chapter will therefore investigate the differing ideas on the causes of the Reformation in the following format:

- Religious factors: heresy – opposition to Church doctrine
- Social and economic factors: anticlericalism and opposition to Church practices
- Political factors: developments in Europe and Germany
- Cultural factors: Erasmus and humanism.

Key dates

1388	The Lollard leader John Wycliffe produced the first vernacular Bible
1415	The Hussite leader Jan Huss was burned for questioning the power of the Pope
1492	Rodrigo Borgia was consecrated as Pope Alexander VI
1503	Giuliano Della Rovere was consecrated as Pope Julius II

1504	Erasmus published *The Dagger of a Christian Gentleman*, which called for a more spiritual approach to religion
1509	Erasmus published *In Praise of Folly*, a satirical attack on the corruption within the Church
1513	Giovanni de Medici was consecrated as Pope Leo X
1515	Erasmus finished writing his Greek New Testament, which was used by Luther to formulate his own religious ideas
1518	At the Diet of Augsburg, the princes of Germany referred to the Pope as a 'hellhound'
1524	Erasmus published *The Free Will*, which rejected Luther's ideas on predestination
1966	The Catholic Church finally removed Erasmus from its list of banned authors

1 | Religious Factors: Heresy – Opposition to Church Doctrine

The importance of religion in 1500

Five hundred years ago the societies of western Europe were dominated by religion. There are three main ways in which we can look at its influence:

1 The way society was organised: In the democracies of Europe today, power lies with the elected government. However, in the Europe of 1500 power was shared between two authorities. Political power was held by the princes, and religious power by the Church, led by the Pope in Rome.

2 The outlook most people had on their lives: Ordinary people in 1500 were deeply interested in 'the next world'. Life on earth was often miserably short. It was generally thought to be just a brief interlude between the infinity either side of birth and death. Child mortality was high, many women died in childbirth, and surviving adults were old at 40. Only fools and the weak-willed were prepared to risk eternal damnation in order to enjoy the fleeting pleasures of sin. For many people the most significant motivating force in their lives was the desire to be certain of salvation, and for this they had to turn to the Church.

3 The reactions of people to everyday situations: We live in a time when most of what happens around us can be explained in **rational** terms. In 1500 this was not the case. Droughts, plagues and other natural disasters were seen as the work of God or the Devil. The immediate reaction was to pray to heaven for assistance. This was not usually done by addressing God directly, for He was thought to be inaccessible to ordinary people. The

Key questions
How popular were the beliefs of the Catholic Church on the eve of the Reformation? Why was religion so important to people at this time?

Key date
The Lollard leader John Wycliffe produced the first vernacular Bible: 1388

Key term
Rational
Taking a logical and scientific approach.

Lollards
Medieval heretics
based in England
who followed the
teachings of John
Wycliffe.

Hussites
Medieval heretics
based in Bohemia
who followed the
teachings of Jan
Huss.

Key question
What evidence
suggests that Church
beliefs were already
under serious attack
by the time of
Luther's revolt?

Scriptures
The sacred written
texts of the
Christian faith.

Devotio Moderna
Literally 'modern
devotion' – a
Catholic movement
based in Holland
which stressed that
a simple devotion to
the teachings of
Christ was more
important than
carrying out rituals.

**Christocentric
realism**
An artistic style
which encouraged
Christians to focus
more on the
teachings of Christ
through a realistic
depiction of his life
and crucifixion.

approach was made through his representatives on earth, the
clergy, or his representatives in heaven, the saints. Everybody had
a patron saint who could be called upon for support – a saint who
shared the same name, birthday or trade. For many people,
especially women, the Virgin Mary was favoured as being
particularly approachable and influential. Martin Luther, when
he was famously caught in a terrible thunderstorm in 1505,
prayed to St Anne, the patron saint of miners (Luther's father was
a silver miner). The obsession with saints was very much a part of
everyday life. People carried tokens of their saints wherever they
went, they prayed to them in church, and they sometimes went
on pilgrimages to places particularly associated with them.

Evidence that the state of religion was unhealthy in 1500

Some historians see Luther's protest as being the final stage in a
long and popular campaign advocated by individuals and
movements, which questioned some of the beliefs and practices of
the Catholic Church.

Individuals: Wycliffe and Huss

Luther came from a long line of reformers who had challenged
the Church. The two reformers who are normally seen as being
Luther's closest religious relations are John Wycliffe (*c.*1320–84)
and Jan Huss (1368–1415). Wycliffe in England and Huss in
Bohemia (part of the modern Czech Republic) had argued that
the structure and the beliefs of the Catholic Church contradicted
the teachings of the Bible. Luther was to do likewise. Wycliffe and
Huss attracted large numbers of supporters who were even
prepared to die for their new-found faith (Wycliffe's followers were
called '**Lollards**' whilst Huss's were called '**Hussites**'). Luther had
the same appeal. More particularly, Wycliffe stressed the
importance of individual access to the **Scriptures** and produced a
vernacular Bible in English in 1388 – over 100 years before Luther
did the same in German. Huss rejected the spiritual value of
indulgences and thereby challenged the authority of the Pope –
the same crime of which Luther was accused at the Diet of Worms.

Movements: the Brethren of Common Life and the *Devotio Moderna* movement

Luther tapped into a long-held feeling that the Catholic Church
needed to get 'back to basics' with more stress on individual worship
based around the teachings of Christ. One example of this was the
Brethren of Common Life, established by Gerhard Groet in the
fourteenth century. Erasmus (see his profile on page 50) was
educated by the Brethren of Common Life. This group inspired the
Devotio Moderna movement which stressed that religion should focus
on inward reflection rather than good works. In religious art too
there was a move away from idealised images of the saints towards a
new focus on the physical sufferings of Christ himself (something we
call '**Christocentric realism**'). Hans Holbein's painting of the
entombed Christ captures this development brilliantly (see page 50).

The Body of the Dead Christ in the Tomb (1521) by Hans Holbein the Younger. In what ways does this depiction of Christ differ from those usually found in churches?

Evidence that the state of religion was healthy in 1500

However, there is also evidence that by 1500 discontent regarding the teachings of the Church was not widespread.

Individuals: Wycliffe and Huss

Wycliffe and Huss – unlike Luther – failed to make a major impact upon the Church. The Lollards were driven underground after their most prominent supporter, Sir John Oldcastle, was burned as a heretic in 1416. The Hussites were somewhat more successful, particularly after Huss's arrest and execution in 1415 for heresy. They gained control of the Church in some, particularly remote, parts of Bohemia. But they were unable to win over new areas to their beliefs. Yet Luther's followers were able to do this. Why was there this difference? Why did Luther's attempts to reform the Church lead to the Reformation whereas Wycliffe's and Huss's did not? After all, they all lived at times when there were widespread abuses in the Church, and they all attracted large bodies of supporters. Part of the answer would seem to lie in the personalities, characters and abilities of the reformers, and in the environments in which they had to operate.

Movements: *Devotio Moderna* and the Brethren of Common Life

The *Devotio Moderna* movement and the Brethren of Common Life could easily have been accommodated by the Catholic Church, since they showed a continued and growing enthusiasm for the Catholic religion. Many Catholic figures closely associated with the Reformation displayed little evidence that they were fundamentally dissatisfied with the Catholic faith. For example, Frederick of Saxony, Luther's staunchest supporter, had a collection of 19,000 holy relics – even though Luther argued that these objects had no spiritual value. This collection included – allegedly – a piece of Moses' burning bush and parts of Jesus' swaddling clothes.

> **Key questions**
> What evidence suggests that Church beliefs were not unpopular on the eve of Luther's revolt?
> Why did Luther's attempts to reform the Church lead to the Reformation whereas those of Wycliffe and Huss did not?

> **Key date**
> The Hussite leader Jan Huss was burned for questioning the power of the Pope: 1415

King Henry VIII of England made a barefoot pilgrimage to Walsingham (where apparitions of the Virgin Mary had supposedly been seen) and was given the title of 'Defender of the Faith' by the Pope – even though he eventually took England out of the Roman Catholic Church.

Ordinary people, too, showed little evidence of being dissatisfied with the teachings of the Church. Most Christian people believed that as long as they were baptised soon after birth, went to **mass** regularly, and received the Last Rites shortly before death, they were guaranteed salvation provided their sins were not too serious. They accepted that they would probably be required to spend thousands of years in purgatory, the halfway house between heaven and hell. The minor torments of purgatory were far preferable to hell where, it was believed, totally unrepentant sinners suffered the continual torture of fire, while being tormented by sulphurous smells and the taunts of devils and demons.

A person could reduce the time which their soul ultimately spent in purgatory by purchasing 'indulgences' from the Church. These certificates, sold on the authority of the Pope, offered a set reduction on the time to be spent in purgatory, sometimes running into millions of years. Many rulers would not allow them to be sold in their territories because the system was open to abuse. However, on the whole, there is little evidence that ordinary people resented them. On the contrary, they probably seemed like a good bargain.

Key term

Mass
The central sacrament of the Catholic Church re-enacting the Last Supper, when bread and wine become the body and blood of Jesus Christ.

A medieval depiction of hell. How does this explain why people felt under pressure to purchase indulgences?

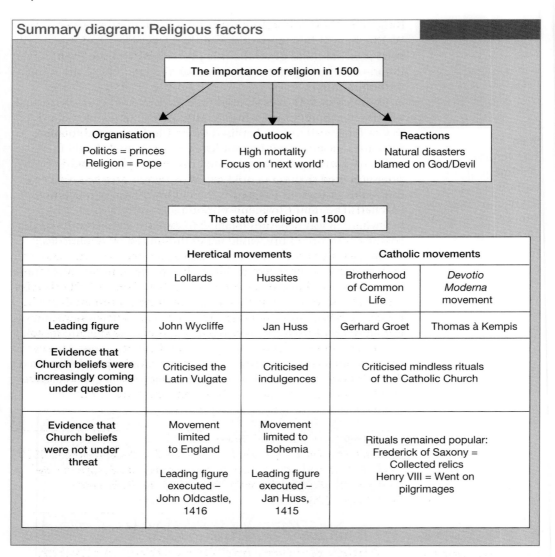

Summary diagram: Religious factors

The importance of religion in 1500

Organisation	Outlook	Reactions
Politics = princes Religion = Pope	High mortality Focus on 'next world'	Natural disasters blamed on God/Devil

The state of religion in 1500

	Heretical movements		Catholic movements	
	Lollards	Hussites	Brotherhood of Common Life	*Devotio Moderna* movement
Leading figure	John Wycliffe	Jan Huss	Gerhard Groet	Thomas à Kempis
Evidence that Church beliefs were increasingly coming under question	Criticised the Latin Vulgate	Criticised indulgences	Criticised mindless rituals of the Catholic Church	
Evidence that Church beliefs were not under threat	Movement limited to England Leading figure executed – John Oldcastle, 1416	Movement limited to Bohemia Leading figure executed – Jan Huss, 1415	Rituals remained popular: Frederick of Saxony = Collected relics Henry VIII = Went on pilgrimages	

The key debate

A question which continues to generate lively debate among historians is:

> Was the Catholic Church healthy on the eve of the Reformation?

For some historians, especially those with a Protestant bias, the Lutheran Reformation was a revolt against a corrupt Catholic Church which had strayed from the true teachings of Christ. As we saw in the key debate in Chapter 1, some of these historians stressed Luther's unique contribution to the Reformation, whilst others were more comfortable presenting Luther as the latest of a long line of medieval religious reformers. Nevertheless, all agreed that the Catholic Church was riddled with corruption and abuses on the eve of Luther's protest. This interpretation of events was substantiated by the research of Geoffrey Elton and A.G. Dickens in their studies of the pre-Reformation Church in England.

Many other historians – Catholics of course among them – disagreed with this interpretation. They point to the Christian humanists, the *Devotio Moderna* and the Brethren of Common Life as providing evidence that the Catholic Church was still open to fresh new ideas and even to criticism on the eve of the Reformation. Heiko Oberman stressed the religious vitality in the pre-Reformation Catholic Church in Germany, and this idea was echoed in studies of the pre-Reformation Church in England by J.J. Scarisbrick and Christopher Haigh.

In this respect, the rupture of the Christian Church between Catholic and Protestant was more to do with misunderstandings and missed opportunities for reconciliation than with fundamental disagreements over theology. Most bluntly, the Catholic historian Joseph Lortz claimed that Luther might have been a Catholic saint if he had known Catholic theology a bit better. More moderately, the Second Vatican Council (1962–65) started a process whereby the Catholic Church acknowledged that it may have made mistakes in the past and that Luther's ideas could be tied to regeneration in the Catholic Church that took place before and after his protest. In this way, the Reformation was increasingly seen as a European event with long-term roots, rather than a primarily German phenomenon tied to the life of one man.

Some key books in the debate:
Joseph Lortz, *The Reformation in Germany* (Herder and Herder, 1968)
Heiko A. Oberman, *The Dawn of the Reformation: Essays in Late Medieval and Early Reformation Thought* (Wm. B. Erdmans Publishing, 1996)

Key question
How popular were the practices of the Catholic Church on the eve of the Reformation?

2 | Social and Economic Factors: Anticlericalism and Opposition to Church Practices

The balance of evidence suggests that **heresy** was not widespread at the time that Luther made his protest. However, there is plenty of other evidence that **anticlericalism** was more prevalent.

Anticlericalism directed against parish clergy

For the ordinary person, the parish priest was a very important and powerful figure. Through the powers given to him by the Church, the priest alone had the ability to administer the sacraments which could guarantee salvation (see Chapter 1). It was also the priest who had the responsibility for delivering sermons every Sunday which would help the parishioners lead virtuous lives. In other words, the priest was largely responsible for preventing souls from going to hell, and for determining just how long they would spend in purgatory before entering heaven.

Key terms

Heresy
Opposition to the fundamental spiritual beliefs and practices of a particular religion.

Anticlericalism
Opposition to the Church based on its abuse of power and influence.

The priest was also expensive. In return for spiritual healthcare, the priest collected from each parishioner an annual tax called the 'tithe'. This was calculated as ten per cent of a person's annual income. The priest used this large sum for various purposes. For example, the whole of his first year's annual income as a priest had to be handed over in full to the Pope ('annates'). The rest was used to pay for repairs and improvements to his church, and to support himself.

Given the importance and expense of having a parish priest, corruption and unprofessionalism in the priesthood was considered unacceptable. Despite this, the Catholic Church was riddled with abuses. Priests were badly educated, poorly motivated, and more concerned with amassing wealth than with the spiritual care of their parishioners. The most important of these abuses were as follows:

- **simony** (sale of church posts or sacred objects to the highest bidder rather than the best qualified)
- **nepotism** (giving posts to friends and family rather than the best candidates)
- **pluralism** (priests holding more than one post simultaneously)
- **absenteeism** (priests being away from their parish for extended periods).

These abuses were by no means new. However, by the turn of the sixteenth century there was a growing feeling that things were getting out of hand and that even the papacy – the pinnacle of power in the Church – was growing increasingly corrupt in attempting to maintain its political position in the face of French and **Habsburg** attempts to dominate Italy.

Key terms

Tithe
A tax paid by parishioners to their priest of ten per cent of their annual income.

Annates
A fee paid by a new priest to the papacy, usually amounting to his first year's income. Sometimes known as First Fruits.

Habsburg
The powerful royal family to which Emperor Charles V belonged and which controlled Spain and the Netherlands; it also controlled much of Italy, Germany and Austria.

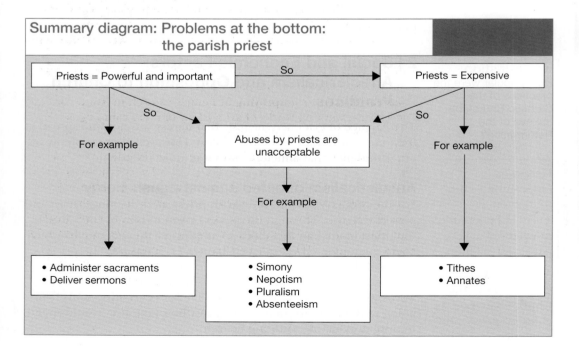

Summary diagram: Problems at the bottom: the parish priest

Priests = Powerful and important — So → Priests = Expensive

So → Abuses by priests are unacceptable ← So

For example → Abuses by priests are unacceptable ← For example

For example

- Administer sacraments
- Deliver sermons

- Simony
- Nepotism
- Pluralism
- Absenteeism

- Tithes
- Annates

Key question
What were the main criticisms directed against the papacy on the eve of the Reformation?

Key terms

Curia
The government and civil service of the papacy in Rome.

Italian Wars
A series of conflicts in which various Italian states, allied with either the French or the Habsburgs, tried to dominate the others.

Papal estates
The extensive territories belonging to the Pope within Italy.

Anticlericalism directed against the papacy

The Pope was the single most powerful and visible figure within the Catholic Church. He had the power to declare new laws in bulletins (papal bulls). He appointed cardinals, authorised the appointment of archbishops, presided over the central government of the Church at Rome (the **Curia**) and even claimed the right to excommunicate kings from the Church if they disobeyed him. He also gathered revenue from the countries in Christendom in the form of annates and indulgences.

The personal integrity of the Pope was therefore essential for the reputation of the Church. There had been occasions in history when particular popes had failed to inspire confidence. However, by 1500 the **Italian Wars** had dragged the papacy into disrepute. This is because powerful families in Italy (in particular the Medici and the Borgia families) got their own candidates elected as pope to further their own interests. These popes were generally cynical politicians who were more interested in increasing their family fortunes than in spiritual matters. For example:

- Alexander VI (1492–1503) invited prostitutes to parties at the Vatican and carved a kingdom out of the **papal estates** for his murderous son Cesare Borgia. He also married off his daughter Lucrezia for political gain – even though she was married to someone else at the time.
- Julius II (1503–13) was known as the 'Warrior Pope' for his military adventures and was condemned in the anonymous publication *Julius Exclusus* (felt by many to have been written by Erasmus). There were also scandalous suggestions that he had sexual relationships with other men. Venetian diarist Giralomo Priuli attested: 'He brought along with him ... some very handsome young men with whom he was rumoured to have had intercourse.'
- Leo X (1513–21) raised a fortune for the Church from simony and from the massive sale of indulgences. Much of this money was earmarked for improving St Peter's Church in Rome, but a great deal went on works of art and on military campaigns connected with the Italian Wars.

The money paid to the Pope had to be raised by princes in the form of taxes on the population at large. So the demands of the papacy were a matter of general concern. The early reformers made much of the fact that the Pope, who was meant to be the good shepherd, devoted much of his energy to fleecing his flock. The massive sale of indulgences across Germany, authorised by the Pope, was regarded by some people as the final straw.

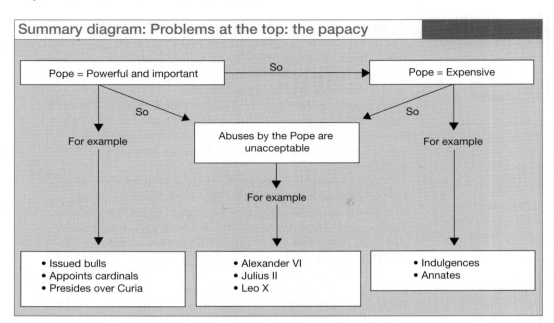

Summary diagram: Problems at the top: the papacy

3 | Political Factors: Developments in Europe and Germany

Key question
How and why did the papacy exploit Germany more than any other European country?

One reason why the Reformation started in Germany rather than anywhere else is because the Church was exploiting Germany more than other nations. By 1500 England, France and Spain had all developed strong centralised governments. This had enabled them to negotiate better deals with the papacy, such as lower taxes and more power over the Church in their own territories. In contrast, by 1500 Germany still lacked a strong central government which could resist the financial demands of the Pope. The 'Holy Roman Empire' was a mishmash of princes, knights, **imperial cities** and an emperor all competing for power and influence (see Chapter 1, Section 1 – 'Important concepts').

Some idea of the administrative chaos of the Empire can be gained from this 1507 account by Quirini, the Venetian ambassador:

> Among the temporal rulers there are two kings, about thirty dukes and an archduke, four landgraves, and a great number of counts … there are five archbishops … twenty abbots, five masters of religious orders, and fifteen priors – all princes of the Empire, who combine spiritual and temporal powers like the bishops … Besides the above-mentioned principalities there are in Germany about a hundred free towns, of which twenty-eight belong to the Swabian League, sixty-two to the great league of Danzig and Lübeck … The authority over the Empire vested in the emperor, or king of the Romans, goes no further than the laws and justice permit, and he cannot despotically force the princes and free towns to obey any particular desire of his …

Imperial cities
Places in the Holy Roman Empire which were not under the control of a particular prince and which represented themselves at the Imperial Diet.

Key term

Key dates

Rodrigo Borgia was consecrated as Pope Alexander VI: 1492

Giuliano Della Rovere was consecrated as Pope Julius II: 1503

Giovanni de Medici was consecrated as Pope Leo X: 1513

At the Diet of Augsburg, the princes of Germany referred to the Pope as a 'hellhound': 1518

Key term

Nationalist
Someone who vigorously defends and promotes their country's language, culture and outlook.

As a result, the power of the papacy to collect taxes, auction Church offices and sell indulgences was impossible to resist. The largest sums were extracted from the German ruling families when they wished to purchase senior Church positions for their younger sons. The amount was especially large if the child was under-age, or already held a position, because such appointments were illegal and required special papal dispensation before they could take place. Vast sums were also raised from the lower levels of society through the sale of indulgences. Huge amounts of money, in the form of gold and silver, left Germany each year to go to Rome. With about one-fifth of Germany under the control of virtually independent bishops and archbishops, there was plenty of scope for lucrative dealings. This was especially the case with the archbishops of Mainz, Cologne and Trier, who were also members of the elite group of seven electors which chose the Emperor of the Holy Roman Empire.

The financial exploitation of Germany by the Church was an insult to German **nationalist** pride. There was a particularly strong feeling that the Church was under the control of foreigners. The Church was headed by the Pope who lived in Rome and ruled over much of central Italy. Each pope was elected for life by the cardinals, the highest rank of clergy. Cardinals, in their turn, were chosen by the Pope. The large majority of cardinals, and nearly every pope, was Italian. In the Diet of Augsburg (1518) the Pope was actually referred to as a 'hellhound'. In the words of the historian John Lotherington, 'This anti-Papalism did not automatically mean the rejection of Catholic doctrine. But it did mean that the enemy of the Pope might well be seen as the friend of the German people.' It is no coincidence that once the Reformation was under way, Luther was depicted as a 'Hercules Germanicus' (German superhero) in the woodcuts of the period.

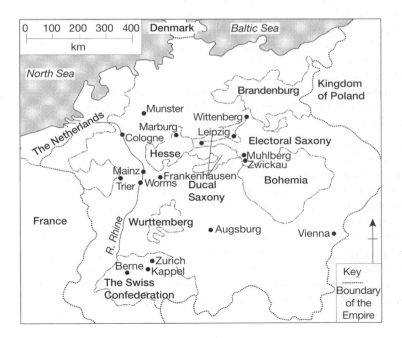

Figure 3.1: The Holy Roman Empire in 1500. What practical problems would face an emperor trying to govern such a wide area?

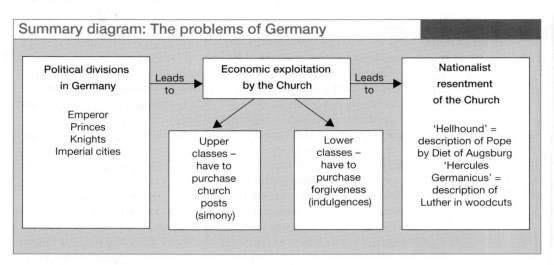

Summary diagram: The problems of Germany

Political divisions in Germany

Emperor
Princes
Knights
Imperial cities

Leads to →

Economic exploitation by the Church

Leads to →

Nationalist resentment of the Church

'Hellhound' = description of Pope by Diet of Augsburg
'Hercules Germanicus' = description of Luther in woodcuts

Upper classes – have to purchase church posts (simony)

Lower classes – have to purchase forgiveness (indulgences)

4 | Cultural Factors: Erasmus and Humanism

The humanist movement, led by Desiderius Erasmus, is often presented as one of the major short-term causes of the Reformation. In fact, it was even said by Cardinal Aleander at the time that 'Erasmus laid the egg and Luther hatched it'. In other words, Luther just rounded off a process which Erasmus had started. Nevertheless, both men rejected this idea and never even met each other – Erasmus said that 'I laid a hen's egg, but what Luther hatched was a bird of a quite different sort' and Luther described him as 'the worst foe of Christ that has arisen in the last thousand years'. On this basis, it could be argued that 'Erasmus laid the egg which Luther smashed'. So what exactly were the similarities and differences between Erasmus and Luther?

Main features of humanism

The **humanists** were scholars who were particularly interested in studying the writings of ancient Greece and Rome to provide practical lessons for life. Central to this idea was that scholars should read the earliest, therefore purest, texts, a notion referred to as *ad fontes* ('back to the original'). This ran counter to the medieval idea of scholasticism, which argued that readers should take the most recent edition, debate and clarify its meanings, and then publish a new version to provide an ever-deepening body of understanding. The aim of the humanists was to discover the meaning that the author had initially intended, rather than accepting interpretations that had been made in the Middle Ages based on incomplete texts and poor translations.

Humanism had become increasingly important in the scholarly world of the highly educated during the fifteenth century as the **Renaissance** had spread northwards from its birthplace in Italy. At its heart was a belief that life in this world need not be viewed largely as a penance to be served by sinful men. Instead, there was a great emphasis on people reaching their potential, pushing

Key question
How fair is it to say that 'Erasmus laid the egg which Luther hatched'?

Humanists
The followers of an intellectual movement which encouraged people to read original texts for themselves rather than accept the interpretations of others.

Key term

Key question
What were the main features of the humanist movement?

Renaissance
The 'Rebirth' of classical learning in the late medieval period which encouraged people to think for themselves rather than blindly accept what they were told.

Key term

themselves to their limits, challenging accepted viewpoints. Rather than meekly accepting established teachings and explanations, the humanists demanded to be shown the evidence. This approach was generally unwelcome in the Church, where the normal requirement was unquestioning obedience. But not all prominent churchmen were hostile to it, because it could be argued that by looking at the evidence afresh one might be able to come to a clearer understanding of God and His will. So the humanists were allowed to continue their researches unmolested as long as they did nothing to challenge the existing power structure within the Church.

Ways in which Erasmus was similar to Luther
Methods used: similar to Luther's *sola scriptura*

Key question
In what ways was Erasmus similar to Luther?

Erasmus was what we call a **Christian humanist**: in other words, he applied the techniques of humanism to the Christian Scriptures. He looked away from the Latin Vulgate (which had built up over the centuries in the scholastic fashion) and towards the earliest Greek (New Testament) and Hebrew (Old Testament) sources from which it had developed. The Christian humanist Johann Reuchlin produced a Hebrew–Greek dictionary; Erasmus used this to produce a Greek New Testament from the original sources in 1515 ('What I read in Sacred Scripture … I believe with complete confidence, nor do I reach further').

Conclusions drawn: similar to Luther's *Ninety-five Theses*
By going back to the original scriptures, Erasmus was shocked at how far the Church had strayed from their teachings and decided that the Church was in serious need of reform. In 1504 he published *The Dagger of a Christian Gentleman*, which mocked the scholastic obsession with ever-narrower detail ('How many angels can dance on a pinhead?') and encouraged more focus on the teachings of Christ ('Make Christ your goal'). His 1509 satire, *In Praise of Folly*, ridiculed the typical churchman by appearing to praise him for his faults. This became the contemporary equivalent of a best-seller. By the time Luther became famous there were thousands of followers and admirers of Erasmus in all parts of Europe, many of whom were in high places. Some of his works were banned by the Catholic Church until 1966.

Ways in which Erasmus differed from Luther
Conclusions drawn: different to Luther's idea of 'predestination'

Key question
In what ways was Erasmus different to Luther?

Despite these similarities, the link between Erasmus and Luther is not so clear-cut. Erasmus shared Luther's anticlericalism. However, Erasmus stopped short of Luther's heresy. Erasmus initially supported Luther when the issue was Church practices. When issues of Church beliefs surfaced, however, Erasmus broke with him. Erasmus felt that Luther's heresy would 'tear the seamless robe of Christ' and lead to terrible bloodshed. Most crucially, in his book *The Free Will* (1524) Erasmus utterly rejected Luther's doctrine of **predestination**. The whole philosophy of humanism

Key terms

Christian humanist A person who applied the techniques of humanism to the Christian Scriptures to get closer to the original meaning.

Predestination The idea that God, being all-knowing and all-powerful, has already decided which souls are going to heaven and which souls are going to hell.

was all about self-improvement (as the Italian humanist Alberti put it, 'Man can make whatever he likes of himself') and therefore free will. Luther rejected this argument whilst praising the eloquence with which Erasmus expressed it ('It is as if rubbish or dung should be carried around in vessels of gold or silver').

Erasmus and many of the other leading humanists refused to join Luther, preferring to remain within the Church and to campaign for change from within. They denied that they were in any sense responsible for what they thought of as Luther's excesses. In 1520 Erasmus wrote to the Papal Legate saying that:

> The corruption of the Roman Court may require reform, extensive and immediate, but I and the like of me are not called on to take a work like that upon ourselves. I would rather see things left as they are than to see a revolution which may lead to one knows not what. Others may be martyrs if they like. I aspire to no such honour. Some hate me for being a Lutheran; some for not being a Lutheran. You may assure yourself that Erasmus has been, and always will be, a faithful subject of the **Roman See**.

This was to remain his position throughout the rest of his life. Two years later in a letter to one of his many correspondents he further clarified his position:

> Each side pushes me and each reproaches me. My silence against Luther is interpreted as consent, while the Lutherans accuse me of having deserted the gospel out of timidity. ... I cannot be other than what I am, and cannot but execrate dissension. I cannot but love peace and concord. I see how much easier it is to start than to assuage a tumult.

Luther thought such a view was completely unacceptable, and was not slow to inform Erasmus of his opinion in very strong language. The two men rapidly lost respect for one another, and, in Luther's case, admiration turned to hatred. Erasmus's feelings were not as strong, but even he allowed his annoyance to show, as in this letter to Luther of 1526:

> The whole world knows your nature, according to which you have guided your pen against no one more bitterly and, what is more odious, more maliciously, than against me. ... How do your scurrilous charges that I am an atheist help the argument? ... Wish me any curse you will except your temper, unless the Lord change it for you.

Erasmus's views were shared by many humanists. Some, such as **Sir Thomas More** in England, were even prepared to die rather than renounce their allegiance to the Church. So it cannot be argued that the Reformation was the deliberate work of humanists. However, inadvertently they provided Luther with the tools which he used as weapons against the Church: the idea of returning to original scriptures, a new (Greek) version of the New Testament, and a ready audience for controversial religious debate. It is on this basis that the German historian Bernd Moeller famously argued 'No humanism, no Reformation'.

Key term

Roman See
The Bishopric (See) of Rome – another word for the papacy.

Key dates

Erasmus published *The Dagger of a Christian Gentleman*, which called for a more spiritual approach to religion: 1504

Erasmus published *In Praise of Folly*, a satirical attack on the corruption within the Church: 1509

Erasmus finished writing his Greek New Testament, which was used by Luther to formulate his own religious ideas: 1515

The Catholic Church finally removed Erasmus from its list of banned authors: 1966

Erasmus published *The Free Will*, which rejected Luther's ideas on predestination: 1524

Key figure

Sir Thomas More
A prominent English politician and writer who was executed by King Henry VIII for refusing to renounce his Catholic faith.

Profile: Desiderius Erasmus (1466–1536)

1466	– Erasmus was born Gerrit Gerritzoon, the illegitimate second son of a soon-to-be monk in Rotterdam
1484	– After his parents died of plague, Erasmus was placed in an Augustinian monastery to train as a monk. He hated it
1499	– Went to England, where he met prominent Catholic intellectuals including Thomas More
1504	– Published *The Dagger of a Christian Gentleman* which promoted a simple Christ-centred religion and rejected mindless ritual ('We kiss the shoes of saints and their dirty handkerchiefs, yet we leave their words, their most holy relics, neglected')
1509	– Published *In Praise of Folly* while staying at the home of Thomas More. This book criticised abuses in the Church and in particular the sale of indulgences
1513	– Rumoured to be the author of the anonymous *Julius Exclusus*, a bitter attack on the corruption of the papacy
1516	– Published his Greek New Testament, dedicated to Pope Leo X. Exposing translation errors in the Vulgate, it also became the text which Luther used to write his German Testament of 1522
1517	– Luther published his *Ninety-five Theses* against abuses in the Church
1519	– Supported Luther's anticlerical attacks upon the Church and sent copies of the *Ninety-five Theses* to Thomas More in London
1521	– Opposed Luther's heretical rejection of Catholic doctrine made at the Diet of Worms
1524	– Attacked Luther's views on predestination under pressure from Pope Clement VII. Luther responded violently in his book *On the Bondage of the Will*
1536	– Died in Basel not long after hearing of the execution of Thomas More for treason

Desiderius Erasmus rose from humble beginnings to become the leading humanist scholar of the early sixteenth century. From his home in the Netherlands he built up a network of correspondents in many countries via which the latest scholarly findings were widely circulating and the issues of the day discussed. His advice was sought by many of Europe's leading political figures. His publications were written in Latin, the language of scholars, and were to be found in all centres of learning throughout western Europe. His reputation as a thinker and researcher was unsurpassed. His speciality was the study of the New Testament of the Bible, and in this he showed the typical humanist approach. He was not prepared to rely on the generally accepted text – the Vulgate, which was a translation into Latin of the original texts –

but insisted on studying the earliest known manuscripts, which were in Greek. He drew attention to the ways in which some of the Church's teachings were based on texts that were in fact mistranslations made by St Jerome, the author of the Vulgate.

One of the greatest contributions of Erasmus was to publish, in 1516, an accurate version of the New Testament in Greek, which other scholars could use in preparing vernacular editions of the Bible (editions in their own languages). He worked to make it clear, to those with the education and intellectual ability to understand, that the teachings and practices of the Church were riddled with errors and inconsistencies. He felt particularly strongly that the Church should be encouraging people to live Christ-like lives rather than teaching them to seek salvation through the practice of empty formalities. In this he was echoing the views of a large but unorganised band of reformers throughout Europe which had been seeking a spiritual regeneration of the Church for at least a century.

Erasmus had a great deal in common with Luther. In particular, they both felt that the Church was in desperate need of reform which would sweep out the errors and inconsistencies which had crept in over the centuries. Luther's own studies of the Bible used Erasmus's Greek New Testament, and in the opening stages of the Reformation Luther corresponded with Erasmus frequently. However, Erasmus fundamentally differed from Luther in two ways: firstly, by believing that the Church could reform itself from within, and secondly by arguing that predestination was a cold and frightful concept which removed any incentive for good behaviour. When Luther drifted from anticlericalism (criticism of Church practices) into heresy (criticism of fundamental Church beliefs) Erasmus came out against Luther in outright opposition and the relationship between the two men broke down.

Erasmus would not have welcomed the suggestion that he helped to create the Reformation. He always preached reconciliation rather than confrontation and deeply regretted the division of the Church into Protestant and Catholic factions. Nevertheless, the fact remains that it was Erasmus and his fellow reformers who provided Luther with the tools which he used as weapons against the Church. In this sense, had it not been for the work of Erasmus and his fellow humanists, the Reformation may not have happened. Although it was not their intention, they helped create an intellectual climate in which Luther's ideas were not only acceptable but positively welcomed.

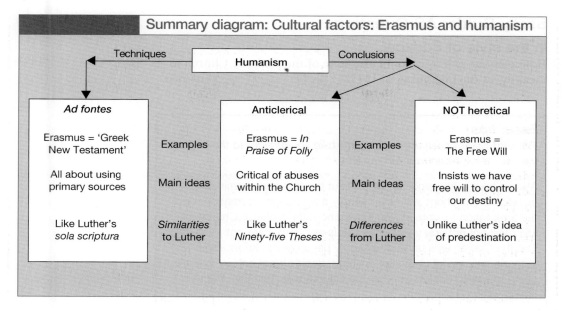

Summary diagram: Cultural factors: Erasmus and humanism

Techniques — Humanism — Conclusions

Ad fontes		Anticlerical		NOT heretical
Erasmus = 'Greek New Testament'	Examples	Erasmus = *In Praise of Folly*	Examples	Erasmus = The Free Will
All about using primary sources	Main ideas	Critical of abuses within the Church	Main ideas	Insists we have free will to control our destiny
Like Luther's *sola scriptura*	*Similarities* to Luther	Like Luther's *Ninety-five Theses*	*Differences* from Luther	Unlike Luther's idea of predestination

Study Guide: AS Questions

In the style of Edexcel

How accurate is it to describe the state of the Catholic Church as 'healthy' at the beginning of 1517?   (30 marks)

Exam tips

The cross-references are intended to take you straight to the material that will help you answer the question.

Always take a little while to think about the focus of examination questions. Questions will never simply ask you for information, so the temptation to write all you know about the Catholic Church in 1517 will not get you very far here. It is also important not to assume that the Church was unhealthy simply because you know about Luther's successful challenge. Instead, decide what criteria you are going to use to decide whether the Church was 'healthy'. Pages 49–55 will help you here.

It may be helpful to think of this issue in terms of human health. You could envisage the Church in c.1500 as a quite healthy person who catches an infection which is not well treated – and hence is seriously weakened by it. Alternatively did the Church more resemble an already sick person too weak to resist?

- In support of the view that the Church was fundamentally sound you could use the evidence of devotion and the widespread adherence to the teachings of the Church (page 52) and the Church's own religious vitality (page 54) in the early sixteenth century. How will you deploy the information concerning the challenge from Wycliffe and Huss? As evidence of challenge to the Church? Or as evidence of its ability to resist challenge? Actually you will need to do both – see page 49.
- In support of the view that the Church cannot be seen as healthy you could use:
  - the evidence that the Church was already under serious attack (pages 49, 60)
  - the extent of anticlericalism and opposition to Church practices (pages 55–57)
  - the particular resentment which developed of the extent of exploitation in Germany (page 58).

This question is a matter of debate amongst historians. There is not a right answer here. Decide for yourselves whether on balance it seems to you that the Church in the early sixteenth century was fundamentally healthy.

In the style of OCR B

Answer **both** parts of your chosen question.

(a) How is the outbreak of the German Reformation best
explained?
[Explaining actions and circumstances]   (25 marks)

(b) Why did Erasmus not break with the Catholic Church?
[Explaining actions, attitudes and beliefs]   (25 marks)

Exam tips

Revise the general introduction at the start of the Exam tips in
Chapter 2 (page 44).

(a) As you construct your explanation, think of building your
argument outwards in layers or levels. Here, you could start by
explaining Luther's reaction to the 1517 indulgence. You could
then move out one step from the *Ninety-five Theses* to establish
the significance of Luther's developing ideas between 1518 and
1520. Stepping out further, you could link Lutheranism to the
wider religious, socio-economic, political and cultural factors
which are all considered within this chapter. The most
accomplished answers will establish links between Luther's
religious standpoint and these outer layers: Luther's attack on
indulgences also appealed to the deeply-held belief that Rome
was robbing Germany of money; Luther's call for a vernacular
Bible also appealed to German nationalists; his attack upon the
authority of the Pope appealed to the princes who wanted more
power within their own territories.

(b) This question takes you to the heart of the confusions and
misunderstandings that were so important in the early years of
the Reformation, but which we do not notice in our search for
neat explanations.

One effective way to answer the question would be to
consider why Erasmus first supported Luther but later broke with
him. In doing that, make it clear not just that the rupture came
slowly, but that Erasmus had never fully supported Luther
anyway. Review the information in this chapter which provides
you with useful points regarding the ways in which Erasmus was
similar to Luther, and the ways in which they differed.

You can thus show that Erasmus remained a Catholic not
simply because he belonged to the older generation and was a
conservative. Erasmus remained in the Catholic Church because
he saw it as the guarantor of the *consensus fidelium*, the

corporate community of the Church across the centuries through which the Holy Spirit made itself known and instructed the faithful. The early battle lines between Catholic and reformer were never clear. Many moderates wanted agreement, not confrontation, but the front lines were hardening. Erasmus criticised and was criticised by both sides, but he was eventually forced to choose between them.

Social, Cultural and Political Impact

POINTS TO CONSIDER

Luther believed passionately in a small number of religious issues. To him they were matters of life and death. Luther wrote an enormous number of publications on these issues which were printed and widely circulated. Never before had so much appeared in print from the pen of one man. The variety was remarkable. There were serious academic works in Latin, closely argued justifications of his position in German, and what were essentially pieces of propaganda attacking the Pope in highly abusive terms, aimed at the common people. Other issues concerned Luther less and he made little effort to publicise his opinions about them until the situation forced him to do so. In the meantime, his views were often misinterpreted, sometimes with catastrophic results. Historians disagree about how far Luther was responsible for what happened, and how far he deserves credit or criticism for the way he reacted to events.

This chapter considers how Luther's religious message was spread and with what results. It also considers the political and social implications of his teachings. The chapter is structured as follows:

- Clarifying and spreading the message
- Impact on politics and society.

Key dates

1520	Luther's three major pamphlets developed his ideas for the ruling classes
1522	Luther's German New Testament provided Lutheran pastors with the raw material for sermons
1529	Luther's *Large* and *Small Catechisms* summarised the essential teachings of the Christian faith
1522–23	The Knights' War: the Imperial Knights rose up in revolt using Luther's ideas to justify political change

1524–25	The Peasants' War: the peasants rose up in revolt using Luther's ideas to justify social change
1525	Luther married Katherine von Bora and began to raise a family of six children
1540	Luther's reputation as a defender of family values was badly damaged when he encouraged the bigamous marriage of Philip of Hesse

1 | Clarifying and Spreading the Message

Introduction

The development of the printing press helped Luther's ideas to spread and to take hold. In the Middle Ages, books were written by hand. They were therefore rare and expensive. But by 1500 the printing press had been invented and a huge amount of cheaply produced material was flooding Europe. This rush of information and ideas can be compared with the impact of the internet five hundred years later.

Because of the printing press, Luther's ideas were able to reach a much larger audience over a much wider area than would have been the case a hundred years earlier. A printing press could produce a thousand books in the same time it took a **scribe** to produce just one. Even so, the technology of the time meant that every page of every copy had to be printed separately and slowly. Despite this, the output from the presses was massive. Between 1517 and 1520 about 300,000 copies of Luther's works were printed. His German Bible sold 200,000 copies in just 12 years. Copies of his works were passed from hand to hand. They were eagerly read both privately and publicly throughout Germany, and especially in the towns and cities, where most of the literate population lived. It took only two weeks for *Ninety-five Theses* to get across Germany and little over a month to reach Thomas More in London.

The most significant of Luther's written works were the 1520 pamphlets, the German Bible and the *Catechisms*. In addition, a number of **woodcuts** – crude cartoons – helped to get the message across to ordinary people. We will now proceed to look at each of these in turn.

The 1520 pamphlets

By 1520 many of Luther's ideas were well developed. During that year he wrote 24 works for publication, including the three that are generally thought to sum up his teaching during the early stages of his career as a reformer.

Key question
How did Luther use different types of publications to appeal to different audiences and to serve different purposes?

Key terms

Scribe
A monk whose job was to produce copies of books by hand. They played an essential role in recording and spreading knowledge before the invention of the printing press.

Woodcuts
Images carved into wood and printed onto paper.

Key date
Luther wrote three pamphlets developing his ideas for the ruling classes: 1520

Key question
What was the essential message of each of Luther's three main publications of 1520?

Key question
How did Luther reject the power of the clergy in *On the Babylonish Captivity of the Church*?

On the Babylonish Captivity of the Church

In this pamphlet, Luther rejected the idea that the Catholic clergy had a special relationship with God. Instead, Luther argued that all Christians were equal in the eyes of God – that there was a 'priesthood of all believers'. Catholic priests drew much of their power and authority from the fact that only they could carry out the seven sacraments (see Chapter 1, page 16–17) which provided the only true line of communication between God and humanity. So, nobody could be saved without the services of the Church, administered by priests.

Luther argued that only two of the seven sacraments – baptism and the Eucharist – were clearly justified in the Bible. The other five were, therefore, invalid. His rejection of confirmation, matrimony and extreme unction had no major implications for the power of the priesthood. Much more serious was Luther's rejection of penance and ordination.

Penance

Through this sacrament Catholic priests claimed they could forgive sins on God's behalf and save people from eternal damnation. Luther disagreed. He argued that the forgiveness of sins was a private matter between the believer and God in which the priest did not have a vital part to play. As a result, the Church had no right to sell indulgences, which were worthless.

Ordination

This sacrament involved a man taking 'Holy Orders' to become a priest. It suggested that priests were an elite group who were separate from and above ordinary people. They could not be subjected to the legal requirements that applied to other people. These special rights were the cause of much anticlericalism in Germany. Luther was convinced that this hatred was justified:

> Of this sacrament the Church of Christ knows nothing: it was invented by the Church of the Pope. It not only has no promise of grace, anywhere declared, but not a word is said about it in the whole of the New Testament. Now it is ridiculous to set up as a Sacrament of God ... that which can nowhere be proved to have been set up by God ... We are all equally priests ... although it is not lawful for anyone to use this power, except with the consent of the Community.

Key question
How did Luther reject the power of the Pope in *The Address to the Christian Nobility*?

The Address to the Christian Nobility

In *The Babylonish Captivity* Luther had rejected the power of the Catholic clergy. In *The Address to the Christian Nobility* Luther followed these ideas through to their radical conclusion by completely rejecting the power of the Pope. More importantly, Luther combined his religious arguments with a demand for drastic political action. This pamphlet was written in German and – as its name implies – was intended to be read by the German princes.

A woodcut of Luther. What techniques has the artist used to encourage us to support Luther?

Its central argument was that popes through the ages had corrupted true Christianity, and refused to correct the abuses that had been drawn to their attention. As a result, it was the responsibility of the princes to take control of religion in their own territories. The Pope's traditional claim that he was the only person who could make changes to the Church was rejected with an appeal to the 'priesthood of all believers':

> It is a wickedly devised fable – and they cannot quote a single letter to confirm it – that it is for the Pope alone to interpret the scriptures or to confirm interpretations of them. They have assumed the authority of their own selves. And though they say that this authority was given to St Peter when the keys were given to him, it is plain enough that the keys were not given to St Peter alone, but to the whole community … all Christians are truly of the spiritual estate, and there is no difference among them, save of office alone … Thus we are all consecrated as priests by baptism …

Luther had clearly abandoned all hope of reforming the Church from within. It would be necessary to impose change from outside. This idea, more than any other put forward by Luther, was to mark the end of the medieval concept of Christendom, and to usher in the modern secular age.

Key question
How did Luther develop the idea of *sola fide* to reject the power of the clergy in *Concerning Christian Liberty*?

Key term

Salvation
The process of being saved from the flames of hell through God's forgiveness.

Concerning Christian Liberty

The third important pamphlet of 1520 developed Luther's idea of 'justification by faith alone'. Many Catholics scoffed at the idea that salvation is to be gained merely by believing in God. If that were the case, they argued, then sins could be committed with no fear of going to hell. Luther was troubled by this argument and so he attempted to clarify his teachings on 'good works'. He argued that anyone with true faith would automatically do good works. Conversely, good works without true faith carried no credit in the eyes of God. Good works brought no **salvation** in themselves. It was the thought that counted.

> As Christ says, 'A good tree cannot bring forth evil fruit, neither can a corrupt tree bring forth good fruit' … so must first the person of the man be good or bad before he can do either a good or a bad work; and his works do not make him bad or good, but he himself makes his works either bad or good … We do not then reject good works; nay, we embrace them and teach them in the highest degree. It is not on their own account that we condemn them, but on account of this ungodly addition to them and the perverse notion of seeking justification by them …

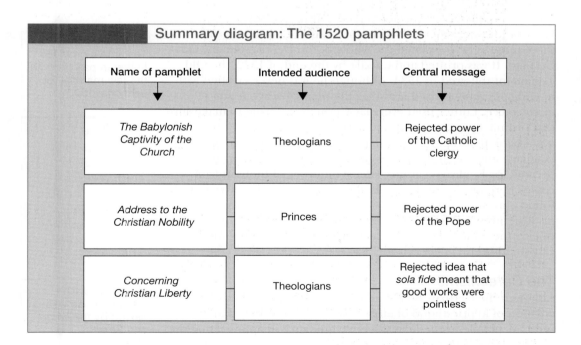

Summary diagram: The 1520 pamphlets

Name of pamphlet	Intended audience	Central message
The Babylonish Captivity of the Church	Theologians	Rejected power of the Catholic clergy
Address to the Christian Nobility	Princes	Rejected power of the Pope
Concerning Christian Liberty	Theologians	Rejected idea that *sola fide* meant that good works were pointless

The Bible

Much of Luther's case for reform as outlined in the 1520 pamphlets was based on the claim that the Catholic Church had strayed from the true teachings of the Bible. So Luther immediately set to work on a German translation of the Bible to prove his case.

There were religious, as well as political, reasons for producing a German Bible. In traditional Catholic worship, the Bible was of very little importance. A few key passages were incorporated into services, but they were read in Latin, which was sometimes not even understood by the priest. It was not thought appropriate for lay people to study the Bible, as they would in all probability misunderstand it. The laity would be told what to believe. There was no need for them to read the Bible themselves.

Luther believed that the role of the priest was to help each person make direct contact with God. To do this, everybody should comprehend the Bible as fully as possible, which meant having it available in language they could understand. There were at least 18 translations of the Bible into German in existence but Luther felt that they contained many errors. He therefore reached an early decision to make his own translation.

When Luther was seized as he was returning from the Diet of Worms, he was taken to the Elector Frederick's remote castle, the Wartburg, where he surrendered his monk's habit and lived under the assumed name of 'Farmer George'. Only his closest associates knew of his whereabouts. But his time was not wasted. In only three months he translated the whole of the New Testament into German. It was printed and on sale by the end of 1522; the Old Testament followed in 1534. Although he was never satisfied with it, and constantly revised it during the next 24 years, it was a masterpiece. Luther used everyday German language to make sure that ordinary people would understand God's message. The result was a book that rapidly became the benchmark for German language and literature, just as James I's Authorised Version became for English a century later. Hundreds of thousands of copies were produced during Luther's lifetime and they were to be found almost everywhere that German was read or spoken. The printing press helped to galvanise German national identity at exactly the same time that it was helping to shatter the unity of Christendom.

The *Catechisms*

Although the German Bible was an essential part of Luther's creation of a 'priesthood of all believers', he was aware that ordinary people needed considerable guidance in appreciating the message behind the words. Luther was an enthusiastic preacher and listening to sermons became almost the central religious activity in reformed congregations. Given the **evangelical** nature of Lutheranism, it is not surprising that most of the sermons focused on portions of the Bible, with clear indications of how their content should guide belief, religious practices and everyday behaviour.

Key question
In what ways did Luther's ideas about the Bible differ from those that were traditional in the Catholic Church?

Key date
Luther's German New Testament provided Lutheran pastors with the raw material for sermons: 1522

Key term
Evangelical
Describes a Bible-based religion which focuses heavily on sermons and preaching rather than rituals and ceremonies.

Key question
What purpose was served by the *Large* and *Small Catechisms*?

Luther's sermons usually lasted more than an hour, but he talked to people at their level while managing to explain some complicated religious ideas about the meaning and mysteries of life, and its relationship to God. More than 2300 of these sermons have survived, and many were published and sold in large numbers.

But Luther and his sermons could not be everywhere. As more and more of Germany became Lutheran there was an obvious need for a clear statement of the central beliefs of the reformed religion so that families and local groups, which were perhaps without an educated priest, could teach both the young and the old effectively. Luther supplied this in 1529 when his *Large Catechism*, aimed at adults, and his *Small Catechism*, for use with children, were published. These catechisms were in the form of short questions and answers about the Lutheran faith. They were intended to be read regularly by each believer, with the most important sections being memorised. It became a normal procedure in Lutheran households for the father to test his family on the catechism every Sunday. Once again Luther had shown his skill and vision in communicating his message.

Although the catechisms were used both in churches and in homes, Luther was disappointed that they were not used more in schools. After all, there had never been such a carefully structured method of instructing children in religion. He was generally unable to convince others that the establishment of schools was a high priority, and he was to continue to complain for the rest of his life about how few German children attended school. It seemed to him that unless something more was done there would be no hope of providing an educated pastor for each congregation. He was right, but it was not until after his death that the issue was seriously tackled.

Woodcuts

The 1520 pamphlets, the German Bible and the *Catechisms* were all important written documents in the development of the Lutheran faith. However, no more than ten per cent of the German population could read at this time. It is true that this minority included the most powerful and influential people in the country. Nevertheless, they would have been unable to carry out a Reformation without the support of the ordinary people. Indeed, in many cases it was ordinary people who pressed their leaders for such changes.

In this respect, it was not the written word but the visual image that was the most important product of the printing presses. These images were known as woodcuts, since they were cartoons carved into wood before being printed in large numbers onto paper. They had the benefit of requiring no or very little written explanation. These woodcuts reached a wider audience and were promoted by Luther 'for the sake of the simple folk'.

Some woodcuts generated positive support for the Lutheran heresy. For example, the woodcut that served as the title page for *The Babylonish Captivity* pamphlet showed Luther as a saintly monk with the dove of peace flying above his head. Another contrasted a simple Lutheran church service with an overblown Catholic service, complete with indulgence-sellers and image-worshipping.

Other woodcuts were negative, anticlerical attacks ridiculing the leadership of the Catholic Church. Such images included:

- the simplicity of the New Testament contrasted with the decadence of the papacy – shown below
- the Pope's sale of indulgences contrasted with Christ throwing moneylenders out of the temple
- the Catholic theologian Dr Eck caricatured as 'Dreck' (German for 'dirt' or 'dung')
- the Catholic theologian Cochlaeus depicted as a 'cock licker' of the Devil.

On the whole, these woodcuts were, in the words of the historian Robert Scribner (1986), 'Like homemade gin – crude, cheap and effective.' However, the simplicity of these woodcuts also meant that their message could be misinterpreted. For example, one woodcut depicted Luther as a violent 'German Hercules' battering the Pope to death with a spiked club. It was particularly designed to justify German rejection of papal power, but more generally it seemed to justify rebellion against established authority. When the princes rejected the power of the Pope, it was inevitable that people lower down in society – the knights, the peasants – would start to rise up against the power of the princes. Woodcuts failed to defuse this explosive situation, and frequently made it worse with their vague messages. On this basis it could be argued that the printing press accelerated the pace of the Reformation, but at the cost of throwing Luther out of the driving seat.

Woodcut contrasting the life of Christ with the life of Pope Leo X; left side, simplicity of the New Testament, with Jesus washing feet of the disciples; right side, decadence of the papacy. What sins did Luther accuse the papacy of committing?

Figure 4.3: Luther satirised as a seven-headed monster – aside from being an ecclesiastic, he is also Barabas the thief, a doctor, an inspector, etcetera. Why was the message of these woodcuts so coarse and unsophisticated?

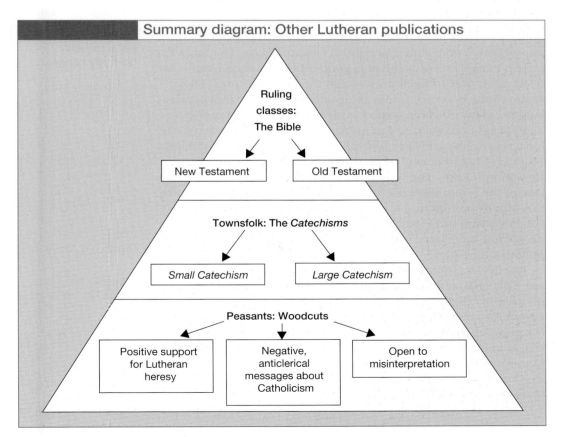

2 | Impact on Politics and Society

Introduction

Luther's views on political and social roles and responsibilities were unknown during the early years of his career. But both his supporters and his enemies made guesses about them. They incorrectly assumed that, because he was violently opposed to the traditional authority of the Pope, he was similarly hostile to established authority in all its forms. So the ruling classes generally feared his influence, and those lower down who were keen for change generally looked upon him as a potential leader.

In fact, Luther was instinctively conservative in political and social matters. At the heart of his thinking was a deep respect for secular authority. Although he violently rejected the Pope's claim to authority in religious affairs, he strongly supported the established authorities in secular affairs. He believed that secular rulers, from the Emperor downwards, received their 'power of the sword' directly from God. They must therefore be obeyed in all earthly matters, even if their actions were unjust (because a bad ruler was a punishment imposed on the sinful people by God). These views were generally confirmed by his studies of the scriptures.

Key question
Why and with what results were Luther's ideas on political and social issues misunderstood?

The Imperial Knights

The Imperial Knights owed allegiance to the Emperor alone. During the early Middle Ages the Emperor relied on their military services to control the Empire. But by the 1500s their importance had declined to relative insignificance. The Emperor was no longer acting as the policeman of Germany. This role had been taken over by local princes and the imperial cities. They resented the presence within their territories of the independent knights, many of whom owned castles and ran private armies. Many knights adapted to the situation and entered the service of local rulers, but many did not. They wanted to see a consolidated Empire with strong central control and the elimination of foreign influence. The foreign domination they disliked most was that of the Pope. They also objected to the fact that the Church, through its bishops and archbishops, was the secular authority in roughly a fifth of Germany. They therefore viewed Luther, when he became a declared enemy of the papacy, as an important potential ally.

The leaders of this group were Ulrich von Hutten and Franz von Sickingen. Hutten was a successful solider, poet and philosopher. Before Luther's 1517 protest he was already well known for accusing the Pope of milking Germany for money. After the publication of the *Ninety-five Theses* in 1517, the knights gave refuge to many German reformers facing persecution from their Catholic rulers. The 1520 pamphlets, in particular *The Address to the Christian Nobility*, appeared to justify a rebellion against established authority.

Key question
How did the Imperial Knights try to use Luther's religious ideas to justify political changes?

Profile: Ulrich von Hutten (1488–1523)

1488	– Ulrich von Hutten was born, the son of an impoverished Imperial Knight
c.1500	– Sent to a monastery to train for the priesthood. He hated the experience
1505	– Fled from his monastery and was disowned by his family
1510	– Wrote an epic poem for Emperor Maximilian which failed to gain a position at the imperial court
1512	– Enlisted in the imperial army as a soldier and contracted syphilis
1515	– Wrote a defence of Johann Reuchlin which established his reputation as a humanist scholar
1522	– Led the Knights' War against the Archbishop of Trier in the name of Lutheranism
1523	– Defeated by imperial forces, he fled to Rotterdam but Erasmus refused to meet with him
1523	– Died of syphilis, alone and secluded at the Isle of Ufenau on Lake Zurich

Ulrich von Hutten was leader of the Imperial Knights during the Knights' War of 1522–23. He is a good example of someone who moved from humanism to Lutheranism and then beyond. He helps to illustrate why so many people initially found Lutheranism appealing, and also why a number of them eventually became disillusioned with what they considered Luther's refusal to follow his ideas through to their logical conclusions.

Ulrich von Hutten was an anticlerical critic of the Catholic Church from a young age. He came from a poor but proud knightly family and – like Erasmus – had been sent against his will to a monastery at a young age. Ulrich hated the dull monotony of the monastic life and ran away in 1505. His father never forgave him, and Ulrich was forced to roam around Europe living on his wits. In the process, Ulrich became just as cynical about the government of the Empire as he was about that of the Catholic Church. Like many impoverished Imperial Knights before him, Ulrich attempted to gain a position at the court of the Holy Roman Emperor. In 1510 he wrote an epic national poem for Emperor Maximilian glorifying the war against Italy, and when this fell on deaf ears he was reduced to enlisting as a soldier in the Emperor's army for a short and depressing period. It was during this period that he caught syphilis, a sexually transmitted disease which at that time was incurable and which slowly started wasting away his body.

It was during these travels – which took him through Cologne, Erfurt, Frankfurt, Leipzig and Wittenberg – that Ulrich came into contact with humanist ideas, which inspired him greatly. In particular, he took a great interest in the Reuchlin Affair. In this case, a prominent Christian humanist had found himself accused of being a Jew by the Catholic Church. This was because he had expressed an interest in going back to original Hebrew texts to get closer to the word of God. Humanists across Europe – including Luther and Erasmus – leapt to Reuchlin's defence with a series of letters accusing the Catholic Church of using intimidation to restrict freedom of information. Ulrich helped to publish these *Letters of Obscure Men* in 1515 and added contributions of his own which helped to establish his reputation as a humanist scholar.

Like many other humanists, Ulrich was a great supporter of Luther's demands for reform of the Church. However, he differed from Luther in two key respects. Firstly, he was more than prepared to use military force to accelerate the pace of reform. Secondly, he thought that reform of religion should be accompanied by reform of the government. These two ideas led to the Knights' War of 1522–23, in which Ulrich led a band of mercenary knights in an attack upon the lands of the Archbishop of Trier. The knights claimed their objective was to spread Luther's ideas into new territories, but most people regarded it as a cynical attempt by the knights to increase their political power. So the princes of the Empire united against the knights, who were defeated in 1523.

Following his defeat, Ulrich fled to Rotterdam in an attempt to secure the support of Erasmus, the most famous humanist of the age. Erasmus refused to see him and Ulrich, increasingly frail, sought refuge in Zwingli's Zurich. He died of syphilis, impoverished and in seclusion on the Isle of Ufenau on Lake Zurich in 1523.

After the Diet of Worms in 1521 the knights decided that the time was right to lead an attack against the territorial power of the Church and in favour of the reformed religion of Luther. They began by launching an attack on the lands of the Archbishop of Trier in 1522. But they had misjudged the situation. The archbishop did not crumble before them, but instead won the active support of other local princes who saw this as an opportunity to break the military power of the unruly knights once and for all. The knights were finally defeated in 1523 and destroyed as a political force. Sickingen fled to Switzerland and Hutten died of syphilis, the public health scourge of sixteenth-century Europe. Although Luther had not been involved personally in the venture, it had been carried out partly in his name. This further convinced many people that Luther's ideas were promoting anarchy.

The Knights' War: 1522–23

Key date

Key questions
How did the peasants try to use Luther's religious ideas to justify social change? Why were they defeated?

The peasants
Causes of the Peasants' War

An even more dangerous situation blew up in 1525. Peasant discontent in Germany had been increasing for more than a century. Landlords and the Church had been gradually imposing heavier taxes and duties upon the peasants. These increasing economic demands coincided in the 1520s with the spread of new religious ideas which suggested that the exploitation was sinful. This created an explosive combination which turned traditional ideas on their head. Suddenly, the peasantry became convinced that rebelling against this state of affairs – rather than humbly accepting it – was God's will. The peasants of Memmingen stated that:

- Since we have been forced to pay the tithe, we think that we should not be obliged to give it any more, for the holy New Testament does not oblige us to give it …
- It has hitherto been the custom that we have been regarded as your poor slaves, which is pitiable, given that Christ has purchased and redeemed us with his precious blood …
- It has been the custom that a poor man did not have the right to catch or shoot game, likewise fish in running water, which is also not permitted us. We regard this as quite unjust and not in accordance with the Word of God, for when the Lord God created man he gave him power over the fish in the water, the birds in the air, and all the animals on the earth …

Main events

Numerous local uprisings in 1524 turned into a widespread general rising in 1525. Although given the name of the Peasants' War, and despite a common symbol (the *Bundschuh*, or peasant's shoe), the struggle lacked unity and central leadership. Hundreds of castles, religious houses and towns were simply ransacked and then abandoned. So it was relatively easy for the princes to re-establish control once the initial enthusiasm for revolt had subsided. They did this brutally, exterminating the leaders and frightening the remainder into submission. They were successful. It has been estimated that perhaps 100,000 peasants were executed.

Key date

The Peasants' War: the peasants rose up in revolt using Luther's ideas to justify social change: 1524–25

Luther's response

Hundreds of Lutheran priests marched and fought alongside the peasants. However, although Luther initially sympathised with the peasants he was soon horrified by the excesses of their actions. So at the height of the crisis he wrote a pamphlet called *Against the Thieving, Murdering Hordes of Peasants* in which he said that it was the holy duty of the princes to 'stab, smite, slay, whoever can. If you die in doing it, well for you! A more blessed death can never be yours, for you die in obeying the divine Word …' He specified three justifications for his verdict:

In the first place they have sworn to be true and faithful, submissive and obedient, to their rulers, as Christ commands, when he says …

Key question
Why did Luther encourage the government to crush the peasants?

'Let everyone be subject unto the higher powers.' Because they are breaking this obedience ... wilfully and with violence, they have forfeited body and soul, as faithless, perjured, lying, disobedient knaves and scoundrels ... In the second place, they are starting a rebellion, and violently robbing and plundering monasteries and castles which are not theirs ... In the third place, they cloak this terrible and horrible sin with the Gospel ... Thus they become the greatest of blasphemers of God and slanderers of his holy Name, serving the devil, under the outward appearance of the Gospel ... I have never heard of a more hideous sin.

Results and significance

Luther's position during the Peasants' War lost him considerable support among the poorer classes. When this pamphlet appeared the slaughter of the peasants was already at its height. The timing of its publication made it look as if Luther was callous and heartless. It was even claimed by his opponents that he was a traitor, deserting those he had earlier encouraged once it was clear which was to be the winning side.

At the same time, the affair firmly re-established Luther's position among the rulers who were inclined towards reform of the Church. Any damage done by the activities of Hutten and Sickingen was more than repaired. He was clearly not hostile to the powers of the territorial rulers, as the Imperial Knights had been. On the contrary, he was suggesting that they were God's deputies on earth.

Key question
What was the significance of the Peasants' War for the development of Lutheranism?

The key debate

The causes of the Peasants' War of 1524–25 is a subject which divides historians.

In the second half of the twentieth century, historians became impatient with explanations of the Reformation which centred on individuals and ruling elites and started examining the contribution of ordinary people. As a result, the origins and significance of the Peasants' War of 1524–25 became a lively topic of debate.

This trend was strongest in the new communist state of East Germany, where historians such as Gunther Vogler depicted the Reformation in general, and the Peasants' War in particular, as a clash between the old feudal aristocracy and an emerging bourgeoisie (middle class). This approach had a long pedigree. The founding father of communism, Karl Marx, had argued that class conflict was the driving force behind historical change. His collaborator, Friedrich Engels, had produced a book which presented the Peasants' War of 1524–25 as an 'early bourgeois revolution' which only failed when the magisterial reformers – Luther included – chose to join forces with the feudal aristocracy to crush the proletariat rather than the other way around.

In western Europe, the interest in the emergence of pop culture and mass protest movements created a similar interest in popular history. In particular, Peter Blickle described the Peasants' War as the 'Revolution of 1525' and as a 'People's Reformation'. However, these historians were less willing than the East Germans to see the Peasants' War as being purely or even primarily the result of class conflict. According to Scott and Scribner – who identified 14 separate causes of the revolt – 'the peasant rebellion was undeniably an anti-feudal revolt, but at the same time it displays frequent hostility towards ... capitalism'. Peter Blickle went further, arguing not only that 'the causes of the Peasants' War had economic, social, political, and religious-legal dimensions' but also that the 'one fixed goal of the peasants [was] the implementation of the godly law and of the gospel'.

Increasingly, historians are acknowledging that the revolt was not a centrally organised uprising but a whole series of spontaneous revolts in which different people in different areas had different concerns. It was an event with no overall leader and no clear list of demands: the Brigach Articles and the Twelve Articles of Memmingen provide us with some general idea of peasant grievances, but they contain such a welter of varied and sometimes conflicting demands that they leave us no nearer to a final conclusion as to the origins of the Peasants' War.

Some key books in the debate:
Peter Blickle, *The Revolution of 1525: The German Peasants' War from a New Perspective*, trans. Thomas A. Brady, Jr. and H.C. Eric Midelfort (John Hopkins University Press, 1981)
Tom Scott and Bob Scribner (eds), *The German Peasants' War: A History in Documents* (Humanities Press International, 1991)

Church government

Key question
How were Lutheran churches governed after the removal of the Catholic Church hierarchy?

Luther's stance during the Peasants' War made it clear that the reformed churches would work with the princes rather than against them. As a result it became tempting for any ruler in Germany, whether or not he was personally committed to Luther's religious ideas, to declare himself a Lutheran. By doing so he could free himself from the political and financial obligations imposed by the papacy and leave himself in control of the Church in his territories. However, the issue remained of how to organise the Church once the hierarchical structure of bishops and archbishops had been removed.

Luther, in fact, was not greatly interested in the arrangements made to ensure the supervision of the Church. His over-riding priority was the maintenance of public order. He understood that the demands of good order necessitated the introduction of some system but he was prepared to accept whatever was agreeable to his leading supporters and the princes.

The structure that emerged clearly established the Prince as the 'head' of the Church within his territories in terms of both protection and regulation. So, in electoral Saxony, the Elector was responsible for appointing a body of 'visitors' who investigated the arrangements and practices of each parish. It was then for the Elector to ensure that the visitors' decisions were implemented. Similar arrangements were made in other states as they adopted Lutheranism.

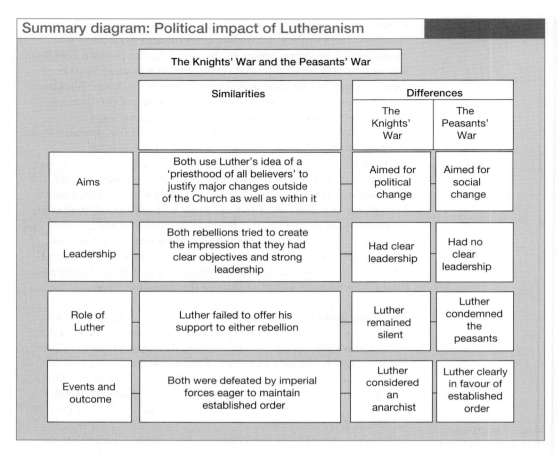

Summary diagram: Political impact of Lutheranism

	Similarities	Differences	
		The Knights' War	The Peasants' War
Aims	Both use Luther's idea of a 'priesthood of all believers' to justify major changes outside of the Church as well as within it	Aimed for political change	Aimed for social change
Leadership	Both rebellions tried to create the impression that they had clear objectives and strong leadership	Had clear leadership	Had no clear leadership
Role of Luther	Luther failed to offer his support to either rebellion	Luther remained silent	Luther condemned the peasants
Events and outcome	Both were defeated by imperial forces eager to maintain established order	Luther considered an anarchist	Luther clearly in favour of established order

The Knights' War and the Peasants' War

Religious practices

Luther adopted the same approach when considering religious practices. While some of his leading followers got very worked up over such issues as images in churches, the vestments of priests, the continuation of monasteries and clerical celibacy, Luther took the view that these matters were '**adiophora**' – of no real importance. He was interested only in those issues that had a direct bearing on salvation, such as *sola fide, sola scriptura* and the priesthood of all believers. The one aspect of church practice which he was passionate about was music, which he regarded as one of God's most precious gifts to humanity. He was determined that its role in church services should be enhanced rather than diminished. To enable this, Luther wrote and published over 20 hymns for congregations and prepared suitable words and music for church choirs.

However, although Luther had little interest in other issues of religious practice, he could not afford to ignore them. This was because others considered them important, and were prepared to cause trouble over them. So he had to take a clear position on these issues. His policy was that if the Bible did not forbid an activity, it should be allowed to continue unless there were strong

Key questions
What were the main changes in religious practices introduced in Lutheran churches? Which of these changes did Luther personally support?

Adiophora
Matters of belief and practice which were not considered of central importance.

Key term

arguments for stopping it. So he was prepared to see images removed from churches if the community considered them a distraction from listening to the Word of God; priests conducting services in everyday clothes if expensive **vestments** suggested they had a special status; and monasteries closed if it was agreed that their incomes could be put to better uses like providing food for the poor and education for the young.

Social practices
Marriage
There was, of course, the problem of what to do with the monks and nuns who left their monasteries and returned to the real world. For the men this was no great problem. The monasteries were self-contained communities of men each of whom developed a useful skill that could form the basis of a trade – accounting, brewing, farming or record-keeping, for example. The issue of what to do with former nuns was not so easy. A typical nun came from a wealthy family which had made a sizeable donation to secure her admittance into the nunnery. It was considered inappropriate for such women to become domestic servants or farm workers, which was pretty much the only work that was available to women at this time. The only alternative was marriage, and strenuous efforts were made to find suitable husbands for as many of the younger ex-nuns as possible.

In 1523 Luther helped a merchant named Leonard Kopp to smuggle nine nuns out of ducal Saxony, which was still Catholic, and into Wittenberg. Husbands were eventually found for all of the nuns except one – a spirited woman named Katherine von Bora. She kept reminding Luther of his promise to find her a husband so that she could stop working as a servant. After two years, in 1525, Luther offered to marry her himself. She accepted, and Luther sent a wedding invitation to Kopp: 'I am to be married on Thursday. My lord, Katie and I invite you to send a barrel of the best Torgau beer, and if it is not good you will have to drink it all yourself.' The Luther household became a focal point for the Reformation in Germany. Katherine coped extremely well with a never-ending stream of visitors and students, while bearing and bringing up six children, raising a further four orphans, running a boarding house for students, and coping with a man who rarely seemed to stop working for long enough to be more than passing company. Despite all of this and the age gap between them (when they married Katherine was 26, Luther 46) the marriage was a happy and successful one lasting over 20 years.

Family relationships
Although many former nuns were able to find a place in society as wives and mothers, their independence and status were arguably diminished. Luther regarded a person's duty to his family as second in importance only to one's duty to God. So, family life was at the very heart of the practice of Lutheranism. He also argued that as the prince was the head of the state, so the father was the

Key question
How can the marriage of former nuns be seen as a successful outcome of Lutheranism?

Key date

Luther married Katherine von Bora and began to raise a family of six children: 1525

Key question
What was Luther's view on the relationship between husband and wife?

head of the family. It was his responsibility to impose discipline on his whole household, including wife, children and servants, and it was their duty to be obedient to him. This did not rule out love and affection, as Luther's many letters to his wife show, but these operated within a clearly hierarchical relationship.

However, Luther's reputation as a defender of conservative family values was seriously dented by the part he played in the **bigamy** of Philip, Landgrave of Hesse. After the death of Frederick the Wise in 1525, Philip of Hesse became the leading defender of the Protestant cause. He suffered from violent mood swings – a womanising socialite one minute, a depressed Christian racked with guilt the next. His family had forced him into marriage as a young man to a woman he found sexually unattractive, but he was at times overwhelmed with guilt over the string of mistresses he resorted to in her place. In 1540 he appealed to Luther for advice. Luther said that divorce was impossible but that Philip could take a second wife if all involved were in agreement. The advice seems to have been based on extracts from the Old Testament. Philip acted on the advice. When news of the bigamous marriage leaked out, the part played by Luther was revealed. His reputation was damaged, and the political position of the Protestant cause was seriously weakened.

Luther had become a petulant (and some would say, nasty) old man. But this should not be allowed to undermine his earlier enormous achievements. It should merely act as a reminder that historical figures are merely human. Luther was a man with faults, failings and inconsistencies. But through the quality of his mind, the force of his personality and the intensity of his religious convictions he was instrumental in changing the course of modern European history.

Key term

Bigamy
The crime of having more than one husband or wife.

Key date

Luther encouraged the bigamous marriage of Philip of Hesse: 1540

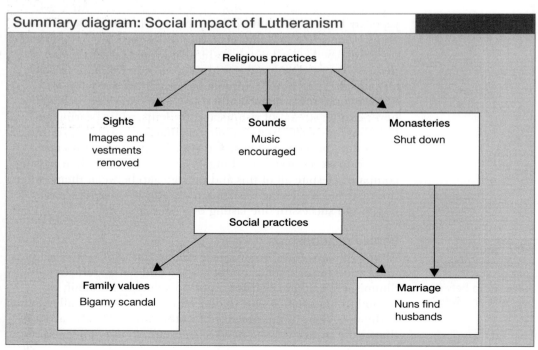

Study Guide: AS Questions

In the style of Edexcel

How significant are Luther's social and political ideas in explaining the acceptance of Lutheranism in so much of Germany? (30 marks)

Exam tips

The cross-references are intended to take you straight to the material that will help you answer the question.

In planning your answer to this question, make sure that you are clear about what Luther's political and social ideas were (pages 76, 79, 81, 83), but resist the temptation to describe them. Instead show how key aspects of his ideas appealed to many of the German princes: his views on the authority of secular rulers (page 80; Chapter 7, page 131); his challenge to papal authority in The Address to the Christian Nobility (page 69); and his conservative views on authority and hierarchies within states and societies (pages 79, 83) including his response to the Peasants' War (page 79).

But other factors were important, factors which allowed Luther's ideas to find widespread acceptance: the resentment within Germany of the Pope's exploitation (Chapter 3, page 58); the development of anticlericalism (Chapter 3, pages 55–57; Chapter 7, pages 128–129); the legitimising of princely challenge afforded by Luther's rejection of the power of the papacy on religious grounds (page 69); and the role of the printing press in assisting the spread of Luther's ideas (page 68).

It is clear that several interacting factors are involved here, but before you come to a conclusion re-read pages 76–78. This will help you think about the crucial role the princes played in Lutheranism's spread, and the importance of the acceptability of Luther's social and political ideas as well as his religious message. You can also find information on this aspect in Chapter 7.

In the style of OCR A
The German Reformation 1517–55

Study the five sources on *The Peasants' War in Germany*, and then answer **both** subquestions. It is recommended that you spend two-thirds of your time in answering part **(b)**.

(a) Study Sources B and C.

Compare these sources as evidence for the danger of rebellion in Germany. (30 marks)

(b) Study all the sources.

Use your own knowledge to assess how far the sources support the interpretation that Lutheranism encouraged social rebellion in Germany. (70 marks)

The Peasants' War in Germany
Source A
Luther, Admonition to Peace, *April 1525*
Luther expresses sympathy for the peasants:

Dear friends, I admit it to be (sad to say!) all too true and certain that the princes and lords, who forbid the preaching of the Gospel and oppress the people so unbearably, have well deserved that God put them down from their seats as men who have sinned deeply against God and man. Nevertheless, you must have a care that you take up your cause with a good conscience and with justice.

Source B
Thomas Müntzer, an open letter to his followers, April 1525
A radical Protestant encourages his followers to violent rebellion:

The whole of Germany, France and the Roman lands are awake. At Fulda four churches were destroyed. The peasants in Klettgau and Hergau are up, three thousand strong, and the longer it goes on the more they are. So now On! On! On! – it is time to hunt down the knaves like dogs. Have no mercy. Do not look at the misery of the godless. Get going in the villages and towns, and especially with the miners and the other good fellows. You shall not be put off by the numbers against you, for it is not your battle but God's.

Source C
A contemporary chronicle, March–April 1525
An account of disorder in southern Germany during the Peasants' War:

Through certain citizens in this town who hold to the heresy of Luther, false teaching has greatly got the upper hand, owing to the deceit and concessions of some of the town authorities.

21 March 1525: Thirty or forty peasants got together in a mob and marched upon the town.

24 March 1525: Someone has knocked off the head of Christ's image on a crucifix and struck off the arms.

20 April 1525: The women run up and down with forks and sticks, declaring that they will plunder all the priests' houses, but are prevented. The citizens are summoned to decide whether they will aid the peasants. The majority decide to send them guns and pikes, powder and lead.

Source D

Luther, a letter to his friends, June 1525
Luther's reflections on the Peasants' War:

What an outcry I have caused with my little pamphlet against the peasants! Everything God has done for the world through me is forgotten. Now lords, priests and peasants are all against me and threaten me with death. Since they are so frantic and foolish, I will prepare myself to be found, when my end comes, in the state that God created me. This should make my enemies even more frantic and foolish before the final farewell.

Source E

J. Lotherington, Years of Renewal: European History 1470–1600, *published in 1988*
A modern historian comments on Luther's appeal to the peasants:

The growing resentment of the peasants found a particular object in the ecclesiastical landlords, mainly abbots, who took tithes as well as rents. In 1525 one grievance against the Abbess of Buchau asserted that every peasant should be 'as free as a bird on a branch and may move to and live in towns, markets and villages unhindered by any lord. She [the Abbess] has forcibly squeezed our freedom from us and has monstrously burdened us with ruin, death taxes, marriage restrictions and serfdom, defying God's decree and all reason and even her own edict of freedom.' Luther's protest seemed like a manifesto of liberation against such ecclesiastical oppression. His call for spiritual equality given 'the priesthood of all believers' was readily extended by the peasants to a demand for social equality.

Exam tips

(a) In a comparison of two sources, you must make direct references to the sources themselves, identify any features that are complementary as well as contradictory, and comment on the nature of the sources' authenticity, completeness, consistency, typicality and usefulness. You are not expected to consider all of these qualities but to discuss the most important. Remember that you should only use your own knowledge to provide a context for the sources and your answer should not be driven by contextual knowledge. Some of the main points you might discuss are:

- Both sources point to the violent conduct of peasants and miners.
- Both refer to urban conflict, Source B taking the fight to the towns and Source C, an account of iconoclasm in German towns.
- In Source C Luther is held responsible for the violence whereas Müntzer in Source B was clearly inciting the peasants to revolt.
- Source B portrays the genuine feelings of the writer whereas Source C is a biased account that is critical of the effects of Luther's ideas.
- Though Luther's ideas were preached throughout Germany, the Peasants' War had its greatest impact in the west and south of the Empire. Violence did not occur everywhere and in many places was quickly suppressed.

(b) The answer requires a good balance between your own knowledge and an analysis of all five sources. Your answer might consider some of the following points:

- Most of the sources suggest that Luther encouraged social rebellion, however indirectly; Source B implies Müntzer was as much if not more responsible.
- Source C is the most direct condemnation of Luther but the account has been written by a biased chronicler who blames Luther for all outbreaks of iconoclasm.
- Luther's accounts in Sources A and D reveal his desire for the rule of law. Source A acknowledges his initial justification for the uprisings and Source D his private anger at how he was unfairly blamed for the violence.
- Source E confirms that Luther's message that 'all men are priests' was taken out of context and misinterpreted by the peasants, implying that only indirectly was he responsible for social rebellion.

In the style of OCR B

Answer **both** parts of your chosen question.

(a) Why was the Reformation supported by the Imperial Knights?
[Explaining motives, actions and circumstances]   (25 marks)

(b) How far do political issues in Germany explain much of Luther's appeal to 1529?
[Explaining ideas, motives and circumstances]   (25 marks)

Exam tips

The cross-references are intended to take you straight to the material that will help you answer the questions.

Look again at the general introduction at the start of the Exam tips in Chapter 2 (page 44).

(a) Good answers will weigh up the relative importance of reasons and the ways in which some are interconnected. The most famous of the knights, Ulrich von Hutten, provides an ideal starting point: show the interaction of strong anti-papal feeling with nationalistic and humanistic tendencies. Read the profile of von Hutten within this chapter to help you here (pages 77–78). Then move on to consider the knights more generally, showing how they were caught in the combined squeeze of long agricultural depression and the growing power of the territorial princes. By now, your essay has moved far from theology, but don't leave things there. An excellent ending would link the knights back to Luther, e.g. von Kronberg wrote pro-Lutheran pamphlets and after the Knights' War converted the Duke of Württemberg to Lutheranism; von Sickingen sponsored major evangelical figures such as Bucer and Melanchthon and, before any prince, implemented a Lutheran reformation in his territory – i.e. to say they used the Reformation for their own ends is too simplistic.

(b) This question is about motives and ideas. Start by considering Luther's political appeal: in other words, how the adoption of his ideas would increase the power and influence of certain members of society. You could use your knowledge of Frederick of Saxony's clash with Emperor Charles V here from Chapter 2, and the more selfish motives of the Imperial Knights outlined within this chapter.

The question, however, uses the phrase 'How far', which means that you are expected to compare the political appeal of Luther's protest with other possible causes for his popularity. For example, there was a social dimension to Luther's appeal: in this context, you could consider the motives of the peasants, covered in this chapter. A cultural dimension to his appeal is provided by a study of the humanists, dealt with in the last chapter. Finally, there is of course a religious dimension to consider. Use your notes from the first two chapters to consider why Luther's theological views on sin, salvation and the sacraments were so appealing. People responded because he offered a different theology of salvation, a way out of the endless struggle to earn their salvation. He cut the influence of the clergy. He promised a direct relationship with God – not a terrifying God keen to condemn but a merciful God keen to forgive. Preaching and pamphlets spread this message and many responded.

In a conclusion, you must make a judgement. Can a single explanation cover the complex motives of so many different people and groups, even within a single 'class'? People attempted to understand Luther, but they also interpreted him to fit into their own environment.

5 Zwingli

POINTS TO CONSIDER

We must avoid falling into the trap of believing that Martin Luther was the only person who mattered in the early Reformation. Luther was the giant whose influence on events was unsurpassed. However, other significant individuals played their part, even though most historians categorise them as 'minor characters'. Many of the 'minor characters' were essentially followers of Luther who led reform in their own localities. But some regarded themselves as being independent of Luther's influence. They tended to resent his assumed superiority.

The 'minor character' with the greatest degree of independent influence was Ulrich Zwingli (1484–1531). This chapter examines why Luther rather than Zwingli became the central figure in the Reformation by covering the following themes:

- Background to Zwingli's Reformation
- The Reformation in Zurich
- Attempts to spread the Zurich Reformation
- Zwingli and Luther: agreements and disagreements
- Reasons why Zwingli is less historically significant than Luther.

Key dates

1484	Zwingli was born, only six weeks after Luther
1499	Switzerland effectively breaks away from the Holy Roman Empire
1506	Zwingli was ordained as a priest at the age of 22 and took up a post at Glarus
1515	Zwingli turned into an anticlerical following the Battle of Marignano
1516	Zwingli turned into a heretic after reading Erasmus's Greek New Testament

1518	Zwingli moved to Zurich after being dismissed from his post at Glarus and started attacking indulgence-sellers
1522	Zwingli rejected the Catholic idea of fasting by organising a dinner of smoked sausages during Lent
1523	Zwingli defeated the Catholic theologian Johann Faber in the Zurich Disputations
1524	Zwingli broke his monastic vows by marrying Anna Reinhard, a Protestant widow, in Zurich Cathedral
1525	Zurich broke with Rome and began to pursue a Reformation of religion
1528	Zwingli persuaded the Swiss canton of Berne to adopt his reforms and join Zurich in a military alliance
1529 June	First War of Kappel: Zurich and Berne attacked the Catholic cantons but the outcome was inconclusive
1529 October	The Marburg Colloquy: Zwingli defeated Luther in a head-to-head debate concerning the Eucharist
1531 October	Second War of Kappel: Zwingli was killed trying to spread the Reformation into Catholic areas of Switzerland

1 | Background to Zwingli's Reformation

The potential of Switzerland

Zwingli was born and bred, and lived almost all his life, in Switzerland, a loose **confederation** of 13 states known as 'cantons'. Although Switzerland was theoretically part of the Holy Roman Empire, there was a long-standing tension between the Germans and the Swiss. The Germans sneered at the Swiss as being ignorant, poverty-stricken mountain dwellers who shamelessly hired out **mercenaries** to the highest bidder. The Swiss resented the arrogance of the Germans and fiercely guarded their independence. In 1499, matters came to a head. The Holy Roman Emperor declared war on the Swiss after they refused to pay taxes to fund his campaigns against France. With French help, the Swiss

Key question
In what ways was Switzerland potentially fertile ground for the spread of Zwingli's ideas?

Switzerland effectively breaks away from the Holy Roman Empire: 1499

Zwingli was born, only six weeks after Luther: 1484

Key dates

Key date
Zwingli was ordained as a priest at the age of 22 and took up a post at Glarus: 1506

Key question
What did Zwingli believe and why?

Key terms

Confederation
A form of government in which national decisions are taken by a central government and local decisions are made at a lower level.

Cantons
The name given to the main administrative districts within Switzerland.

Mercenaries
Soldiers for hire. Because the Swiss had so little agricultural land, they hired out mercenaries to raise money to pay for grain.

City-state
A city which runs its own affairs and is subject to no outside authority.

defeated the Emperor and effectively broke away from the Empire altogether. So, there was a natural tendency for each group to reject the opinions of the other, which helps to explain why an independent Reformation took place in Switzerland.

Zwingli's beliefs

Ulrich Zwingli was born in 1484, just six weeks after Luther. He was the son of the mayor of Wildhaus, which lay high in the Swiss mountains. Zwingli went to school in Bern and Basel, and entered the University of Vienna at the age of 14. He was ordained as a priest in 1506 and at the age of 22 became the pastor of Glarus. Here, he continued his humanist studies and became fluent in Latin, Greek and Hebrew.

Two events helped to turn Zwingli into a reformer. The first was the Battle of Marignano (1515), in which 6000 young Swiss mercenaries were slaughtered in the service of the Pope. Zwingli, who was present at the battle as a chaplain, returned home convinced that 'selling blood for gold' was not only a waste of human life, but was also corrupting men's souls through greed. Zwingli preached passionately: 'We are already contaminated. Religion is in danger of ceasing amongst us. We despise God as if he were an old sleepy dog…' These were brave words. With no agricultural land to speak of, the Swiss relied upon selling their military service to buy the grain that prevented them from starving. Before long, Zwingli was dismissed from his post at Glarus. But he remained deeply concerned about the negative effect that the Pope's influence was having over the Swiss people.

The second event was Erasmus's Greek New Testament (1516). Like Luther, Zwingli was deeply inspired by the experience of reading the Bible for himself in a 'purer' version than the Latin Vulgate. He memorised large sections of the New Testament and was shocked at how far the Church seemed to have strayed from the Word of God. Before long, he had moved from a position of anticlericalism to one of heresy. Like Luther, he felt that faith alone (*sola fide*) assured salvation, and that scripture alone (*sola scriptura*) provided the means of searching for that faith.

The potential of Zurich

In 1518 Zwingli moved to Zurich, the most powerful of the Swiss cantons, where he was to remain until his death. Zurich was essentially a **city-state** which had acquired large areas of the surrounding countryside by conquest. Zwingli's influence in Zurich was potentially immense if he could convince people of his views, because:

- Zurich was ruled by an elected council. The council claimed control over all aspects of life, including religion.
- Zwingli was given a job as a preacher. His sole duty was to teach the people.

- The citizens of Zurich (like the prosperous inhabitants of most German cities) were independently minded, especially over religious matters. At the time when Zwingli arrived in the city, the citizens resented the Pope for being slow to pay for the mercenary troops he had recently hired from Zurich.

Zwingli immediately began to challenge the **orthodox** teachings of the Church following the arrival of the indulgence-seller Bernadin Samson in Switzerland. Traditionally preachers had proclaimed the teachings of the Church, but Zwingli concentrated entirely on explaining the Bible. He was not afraid to point out where the teachings of the Church appeared to be at fault. He rapidly built up a large following among all classes of the population, including the rich and the powerful. He became a councillor, and within a short time a majority of the council supported his views.

Key term

Orthodox
The established version of the truth.

Key dates

Zwingli turned into an anticlerical following the Battle of Marignano: 1515

Zwingli turned into a heretic after reading Erasmus's Greek New Testament: 1516

Zwingli moved to Zurich after being dismissed from his post at Glarus and started attacking indulgence-sellers: 1518

Summary diagram: Background to Zwingli's Reformation

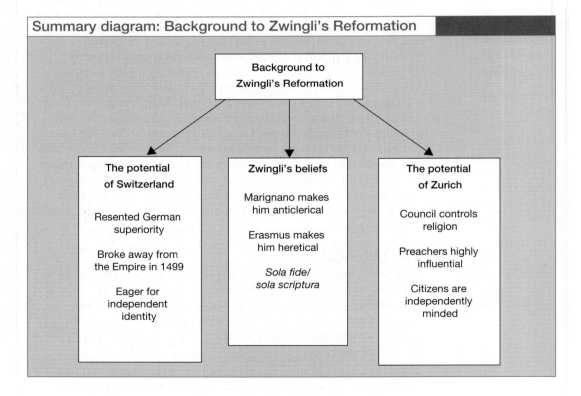

Profile: Ulrich Zwingli (1484–1531)

1484	– Zwingli was born, only six weeks after Luther
1506	– Ordained as a priest at the age of 22
1529	– The Marburg Colloquy: Zwingli met Luther in a head-to-head debate concerning the Eucharist
1531	– Second War of Kappel: Zwingli was killed trying to spread the Reformation into Catholic areas of Switzerland

Zwingli had a great deal in common with Luther. In terms of beliefs Zwingli shared Luther's commitment to the twin principles of *sola fide* and *sola scriptura*. In terms of Church practices, both men were 'magisterial' rather than 'popular' reformers. In other words, they felt that change should be carried out methodically and gradually by the local magistrates rather than left in the hands of the ordinary population. Following from this, both men stressed the importance of education as a tool for spreading Reformation ideas – sermons, pamphlets and public debates, for example. As we shall see in Chapter 6, both men were deeply hostile towards the Radical Reformers, who saw religious change as being the first step towards social and political revolution and whipped up local populations into a frenzy. Finally, in terms of presentation Zwingli shared Luther's showmanship and was capable of making grand gestures to capture the public imagination. For example, in 1522 he organised the famous 'Sausage Sunday' when he broke the Catholic ban on meat-eating during Lent by organising a lunch of smoked sausages (he was making the point that the Bible imposes no such ban). Two years later he not only broke his priestly vows by marrying a local widow, but celebrated the event in a sumptuous service in the cathedral at Zurich.

However, Zwingli's significance for historians is based not on his similarities to Luther, but the distinctions between the two men. Firstly, in terms of practice, Zwingli was the first magisterial reformer to show that the Reformation could work outside of Germany. In other words, Luther's protest was not just a localised revolt owing its success to the bitterness that the Germans felt with the Pope. Rather, it had the strength and momentum to spread right across Europe.

Secondly, in terms of belief, Zwingli was the first magisterial reformer to suggest that Luther's theology was open to question. He even defeated Luther in a head-to-head debate in 1529 – the famous Marburg Colloquy. This was of major significance. Luther was an intellectual heavyweight, a debating champion who had defeated the greatest minds of the Catholic Church – Cardinal Cajetan and Johann Eck. This had created the impression that his theology was somehow above criticism. It had also attracted to Luther a group of disciples who were happy to accept his interpretation of the Bible (quite literally) as the gospel truth. Any reformers who dared to question Luther's judgement were dismissed as idiots, lunatics or devil-worshippers. On the positive side, this gave the early reform movement a great deal of unity and focus. More negatively, it encouraged an almost mindless devotion to Luther's personal teachings. This ran completely against the spirit of a church based on individual faith. Zwingli, by exposing the weaknesses of some of Luther's arguments, showed that the fragmentation of the Christian Church was not going to be limited to only two pieces.

Zwingli himself was killed in battle whilst trying to spread his Reformation into other parts of Switzerland. His body was mutilated, burned and the ashes mixed with dung before being scattered by his Catholic enemies. His ideas did not fare much better – the reform process he had started in Zurich was swallowed up by the Calvinist Reformation later in the century. Nevertheless, Zwingli deserves recognition for being the first man to successfully challenge the authority of Luther. By so doing, he undermined the unity of the reform movement in the short term, but rejuvenated it with intellectual vitality in the long term.

2 | The Reformation in Zurich

Stage 1: Education

From the outset Zwingli argued that violence should not be used against those who rejected his interpretation of the Bible. Persuasion must be relied on at all times, because the uninformed could not be blamed for their state of ignorance. Therefore changes in religious practice were only brought about slowly in Zurich as Zwingli gradually educated people through his interpretation of the Bible. In 1522, for example, he pointed out that the Catholic ban on eating meat during Lent had no Biblical basis, and brought attention to the point by attending a Sunday dinner where two smoked sausages were eaten during Lent. But by 1523 the **Zwinglians** realised that these sorts of theatrics were not generating sufficient opposition to Catholicism, and the Catholics too were keen to have a more direct confrontation with their opponents.

Stage 2: Debate

So the Council of Zurich organised a public debate between the Catholics and the Zwinglians in order to decide which religious path should be followed by the city. The representatives of the Catholic Church refused the invitation to attend the debate, stating that laymen had no authority to decide on religious matters. This left the way clear for Zwingli who was able to set out his beliefs (subsequently published as the *Sixty-seven Theses*) almost unopposed.

Stage 3: Reformation

Within Zurich the Reformation took place with general support and without social or political upheaval. The two principles which lay behind every change were:

Key question
What form did the Reformation in Zurich take?

Key dates

Zwingli rejected the Catholic idea of fasting by organising a dinner of smoked sausages during Lent: 1522

Zwingli defeated the Catholic theologian Johann Faber in the Zurich Disputations: 1523

Key term

Zwinglians
Followers of the reformer Ulrich Zwingli, who was based in Zurich.

- The Bible was the only source of religious authority.
- Its interpretation was for the elected government to decide on.

So, with a maximum of agreement and a minimum of disruption:

- Altars, images and paintings were removed from churches (a process known as **iconoclasm**).
- Priests were encouraged to marry (Zwingli himself married in 1524).
- The rules on fasting were abandoned.
- The **veneration** of the Virgin Mary and the saints ceased.
- Monasteries were closed and their incomes were diverted to charities.
- The council, not the Church, became the final judge in all religious matters.

Stage 4: Schism

What had started out in 1518 as an attempt to bring about the reform of the Church had now reached the point where a break with Rome – in other words, a schism – was unavoidable. The break came officially in 1525 when the mass was replaced with a simple service that took place only four times a year rather than every Sunday. This was unacceptable to the Pope. The rupture would have come sooner, but the papacy had been distracted by Luther and had not wished to alienate one of its few reliable political and military allies.

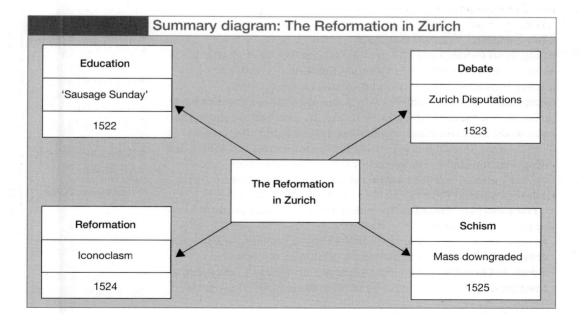

Summary diagram: The Reformation in Zurich

Education	
'Sausage Sunday'	
1522	

Debate	
Zurich Disputations	
1523	

The Reformation in Zurich

Reformation	
Iconoclasm	
1524	

Schism	
Mass downgraded	
1525	

3 | Attempts to Spread the Zurich Reformation

Key question
Why did the attempts to spread the Zurich Reformation meet with so little success?

Unfortunately for Zwingli, most of the other cantons in the Swiss confederation refused to support his teachings. This put Zwingli in a difficult position. He believed that his teachings were essential to prevent people from going to hell. If evangelical preachers from Zurich were prevented from preaching the true message of the Bible in other Swiss cantons then they would not be able to save the people from eternal damnation.

This was unacceptable to Zwingli and the main political figures in Zurich. In 1528 Berne, the other leading Swiss canton, joined the ranks of the reformers. Now only about one-third of the Swiss population lived in the cantons which had remained Catholic. In order to save the souls of the misguided, Zwingli became convinced that evangelical preachers must be allowed to do their work in all parts of the confederation, and that, if necessary, military force should be used to ensure it.

The First War of Kappel

The Catholic cantons refused to be intimidated and successfully set about finding foreign allies to support them. Despite Zwingli's persuasive powers, there was little enthusiasm in Zurich, and less in Berne, for starting a **civil war**. This was shown in June 1529 when war was declared, known as the First War of Kappel. For a month the opposing armies faced each other, taking care to remain just inside their respective territories. The prospect of spilling one another's blood was enough to convince them that the best thing to do was to make peace and try to find a solution to the problem through compromise.

Key term

Civil war
A war between people of the same nationality.

The Second War of Kappel

Peace between the two sides proved impossible. Neither side was prepared to give way and in October 1531 the Second War of Kappel broke out. The Protestant cantons were militarily unprepared and were surprised by a speedy attack organised by the numerically inferior Catholic forces. In what was no more than a skirmish, the Protestant armies were crushed and the war was over. Zwingli, one of many preachers in attendance, was killed. His corpse was mutilated, quartered by the public hangman, mixed with pig entrails, burnt to ashes and then mixed with dung by the Catholic soldiers.

The historian Myconius described Zwingli's death at the War of Kappel:

> Three times Zwingli was thrown to the ground by the advancing forces, but in each case he stood up again. On the fourth occasion, a spear reached his chin and he fell to his knees saying: 'They can kill the body, but not the soul.'

Key dates

Zwingli persuaded the Swiss canton of Berne to adopt his reforms and join Zurich in a military alliance: 1528

First War of Kappel: Zurich and Berne attacked the Catholic cantons but the outcome was inconclusive: June 1529

Second War of Kappel: Zwingli was killed trying to spread the Reformation into Catholic areas of Switzerland: October 1531

Heinrich Bullinger, Zwingli's successor and son-in-law, adds these details:

> On the battlefield, not far from the line of attack, Mr Ulrich Zwingli lay under the dead and wounded. While men were looting … he was still alive, lying on his back, with his hands together as if he was praying, and his eyes looking upwards to heaven. So some approached who did not know him and asked him, since he was so weak and close to death (for he had fallen in combat and was stricken with a mortal wound), whether a priest should be fetched to hear his confession. Zwingli shook his head, said nothing and looked up to heaven. Later they told him that if he was no longer able to speak or confess he should yet … call on the beloved saints to plead to God for grace on his behalf. Again Zwingli shook his head and continued gazing straight up to heaven. At this the Catholics grew impatient, cursed him and said that he was one of the obstinate heretics and should get what he deserved. Then Captain Fuckinger of Unterwalden appeared and in exasperation drew his sword and gave Zwingli a thrust from which he at once died.

With the confrontational Zwingli now dead, Zurich accepted that each canton should be allowed to make its own religious arrangements. In this way, the expansion of the Zwinglian Reformation was halted. It lived on in northern Switzerland, and in neighbouring areas of southern Germany, before being largely overshadowed by the spread of the **Calvinist** movement in the second half of the century.

Key term

Calvinists
Followers of the reformer John Calvin, who was based in Geneva.

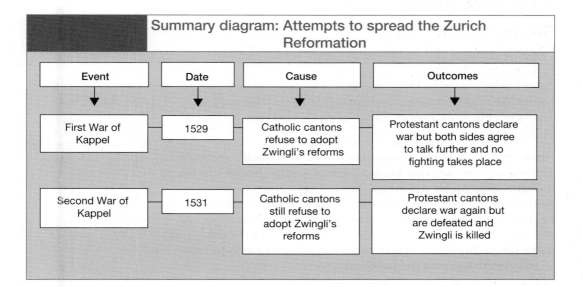

Summary diagram: Attempts to spread the Zurich Reformation

Event	Date	Cause	Outcomes
First War of Kappel	1529	Catholic cantons refuse to adopt Zwingli's reforms	Protestant cantons declare war but both sides agree to talk further and no fighting takes place
Second War of Kappel	1531	Catholic cantons still refuse to adopt Zwingli's reforms	Protestant cantons declare war again but are defeated and Zwingli is killed

4 | Zwingli and Luther: Agreements and Disagreements

Main areas of agreement: *sola fide/sola scriptura*

When Zwingli first emerged as a reformer and began publishing pamphlets to explain his views, he was labelled by his opponents as a Lutheran heretic. His insistence that salvation was secured by faith alone, and that the Bible was the true source of God's will, directly matched the ideas of Luther. It was assumed that he had been converted by Luther's arguments and was one of the many disciples who were spreading the new beliefs throughout the German-speaking world. Zwingli was greatly offended by this assumption. He maintained that he had reached his conclusions independently. He recognised that there were many points of similarity but argued that these were purely coincidental. He claimed that when he first came to Zurich he:

> ... set forth how I would, if God willed, preach the Gospel written by Matthew without human additions or controversial comment. No one here knew anything about Luther except that something had been published by him about indulgences.

He later asked bitterly:

> Why did the Roman cardinal and representatives who were staying at that time in our city of Zurich begin to hate and want to ensnare me, not making me out to be a Lutheran until they knew that Luther was a heretic?

He argued that:

> I began to preach before ever I heard Luther's name, and to that end I began to learn Greek ten years ago in order that I might know the teachings of Christ from the original sources. The Papists say, 'You must be Lutheran, you preach just as Luther writes.' I answer, 'I preach just as Paul writes, why not call me a Pauline?' ... I will not bear Luther's name for I have read little of his teaching and have often intentionally refrained from reading his books. I will have to name but that of my captain, Christ, whose soldier I am, yet I value Luther as highly as any man alive.

Historians have not been totally convinced by Zwingli's arguments. There is no evidence that Luther knew of Zwingli before his own thoughts were highly developed, but Zwingli came into some contact with Luther's ideas and would have found it difficult not to be influenced by them. However, Zwingli claimed, not very convincingly, that his thinking owed nothing at all to Luther – partly due to pride, but also in order to appeal to the Swiss sense of independence from the Germans.

Main area of disagreement: the Eucharist

Although Zwingli's key ideas of *sola fide* and *sola scriptura* had already been developed by Luther, it is unfair to say that Zwingli had no original ideas of his own. Even if Luther had not existed, Zwingli probably would have followed the reforming path he did.

Key questions
How successful were the efforts made to resolve the dispute between Luther and Zwingli? To what extent was Zwingli influenced by Luther's thinking?

Key question
To what extent did Luther and Zwingli disagree over the Eucharist?

Moreover, the fact remains that Zwingli completely disagreed with Luther about the true nature of the Eucharist (the sacrament of the Last Supper, otherwise known as the Mass or Holy Communion).

Issues of practice: agreement

In terms of how the Eucharist was practised, Luther and Zwingli agreed that the Catholic Church had got it wrong. In the Catholic Church, the priest said a prayer over the bread and wine. He then partook of both, but offered only the bread to the congregation. For Luther and Zwingli, this ran against the spirit of a 'priesthood of all believers' in which everyone was equal before God. So, in Lutheran and Zwinglian churches, the congregation partook of both the bread and the wine ('Communion in both kinds').

Issues of belief: disagreement

However, in terms of what actually happened during the Eucharist, Luther and Zwingli fundamentally disagreed. The dispute concerned the meaning of a phrase in the Bible, where Jesus reportedly said when he broke the bread at the Last Supper, 'Eat, this is my body.'

Catholics believed that the phrase should be taken literally. So, the prayer of the priest physically transformed the bread and wine into the actual flesh and blood of Jesus Christ (an idea known as **transubstantiation**). To mere mortals it may still look like bread and wine, but a miraculous change has nevertheless taken place.

Zwingli argued that the words had been used **figuratively** – that by 'is', Jesus had meant 'represents'. For him, the Eucharist was a simple ceremony that encouraged the congregation to reflect on the sacrifice made by Jesus to save us from our sins. Because of this, churches in Zurich only celebrated the Eucharist four times a year (in Catholic churches it took place daily; in Lutheran ones, at least once a week).

Luther was caught between the two positions. On the one hand, he was unwilling to accept the Catholic view, since it suggested that the priest had magical powers denied to ordinary laymen. But on the other hand he was so emotionally attached to the ceremony that he could not accept Zwingli's argument – which was that the Eucharist was a purely symbolic service with no 'real presence' of Christ in the bread and wine at all. Instead, Luther developed a rather complicated theory suggesting that the bread and wine absorbed – rather than were transformed into – the body and blood of Christ (an idea known as **consubstantiation**). The comparison used by Luther was that of an iron glowing in a fire: it is still iron, but it has absorbed the fire.

Results of these disagreements

In the mid-1520s both sides set out their points of view in publications which were distributed throughout the German-speaking world. Luther, as usual, laced his theological argument with large helpings of personal abuse aimed directly at Zwingli ('He is seven times more dangerous than when he was a Papist …

Key terms

Transubstantiation
The Catholic idea that the bread and the wine are physically transformed into the body and blood of Christ during the ceremony of the Eucharist.

Figuratively
Symbolically or metaphorically.

Consubstantiation
Luther's idea that Christ's body and blood are absorbed into, rather than replace, the bread and the wine during the ceremony of the Eucharist.

Zwinglians are fools, asses and deceivers … before I drink wine with the Swiss I would rather drink blood with the Pope'). In response Zwingli was markedly more restrained, and concentrated on the points at issue, although he made it clear that he regarded Luther's arguments as being absurd, illogical and inconsistent. The longer the dispute lasted, the more stubborn the two sides became. Luther accused Zwingli of practising an empty ceremony. Zwingli accused Luther of **cannibalism**. And the more Zwingli seemed to be having the better of the argument, the more stubborn Luther became.

Cannibalism
The act of one human eating the flesh of another.

Key term

The search for a compromise: Philip of Hesse

The leading peacemaker was Philip of Hesse, whose lands lay on the border between Lutheran and Zwinglian territories. He was eager to see the Protestants display a fully united front to Charles V and the Catholic princes to deter them from attempting to destroy the reformed churches with military might. Philip knew that the Protestants would stand little chance if they allowed themselves to be picked off one by one. But Philip's sense of political and military realism was not shared by Luther and Zwingli, each of whom was convinced that only his interpretation of the Bible was in accordance with God's wishes. Each was prepared to change his opinion if he could be convinced that he was wrong, but would not consider doing so for reasons of political convenience. They both thought that, even if a failure to agree increased the chances of meeting a violent and early death in this life, it was preferable to risking eternal damnation.

Key question
Why was Philip of Hesse so keen for Luther and Zwingli to resolve their differences?

The failure of compromise: the Colloquy of Marburg

In a final attempt to gain agreement, Philip of Hesse persuaded the two men, along with a handful of leading supporters, to meet each other. The meeting took place in October 1529 in Philip's castle at Marburg, and the hope was that once Luther and Zwingli were face to face they would be able to argue through the issue that separated them and reach a common understanding. But Philip was to be disappointed. Neither reformer was able to convince the other. Nor were they prepared to accept that the other could be recognised as a 'good Christian'. The meeting, known as the Colloquy of Marburg, was largely a failure. It broke up after only four days and Luther even refused to shake hands with Zwingli before he parted.

Luther wrote a letter to his wife after the meeting which indicates where the major difficulty lay:

Key question
What was the outcome of the Colloquy of Marburg?

The Marburg Colloquy: Zwingli defeated Luther in a head-to-head debate concerning the Eucharist: October 1529

Key date

> Our friendly conference at Marburg is now at an end and we are in perfect union in all points except that our opponents insist that there is simply bread and wine in the Lord's Supper, and that Christ is only in it in a spiritual sense. Today the Landgrave [Philip of Hesse] did his best to make us united, hoping that even though we disagreed yet we should hold each other as brothers and members of Christ. He worked hard for it, but we would not call them brothers or members of Christ, although we wish them well and desire to remain at peace.

Zwingli gave a different impression in a letter he wrote to one of his supporters:

> [We] entered the arena in the presence of the Landgrave and a few others – 24 at most; we fought it out in this and in three further sessions, thus making four in all in which, with witnesses, we fought our winning battle. Three times we threw at Luther the fact that he had at other times given a different explanation from the one he was now insisting on of those ridiculous ideas of his … but the dear man had nothing to say in reply – except, 'You know, Zwingli, that all the ancient writers have again and again changed their interpretations of passages of scripture as time went on and their judgement matured.' … These are examples of his countless inconsistencies, absurdities and follies; but we refuted him so successfully that [Philip of Hesse] himself has now come down on our side, though he does not say so in the presence of some of the princes … [He] has given permission for our books to be read with **impunity**, and in future will not allow bishops who share our views to be ejected from their place. ... The truth prevailed so clearly that if ever a man was beaten in this world, it was Luther – for all his arrogance and stubbornness – and everyone witnessed it, too, although of course the judge was discreet and impartial. Even so, Luther kept on exclaiming that he hadn't been beaten etc.

Yet there were positive outcomes from the colloquy. Positive agreement had been reached on all aspects of belief apart from the nature of the presence of Jesus during the Lord's Supper, and although Luther had refused to accept the Zwinglians as proper Christians, he had undertaken not to attack them in print. So at least Philip had the comfort of knowing that his fellow Protestants would not be at each other's throats.

Key term

Impunity
Freedom from punishment of any kind.

Luther (on the right) disputes with Zwingli at the Marburg Colloquy. What did they disagree about? Why was this disagreement significant?

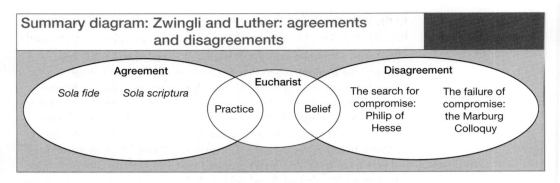

Summary diagram: Zwingli and Luther: agreements and disagreements

Agreement
Sola fide   Sola scriptura

Eucharist
Practice   Belief

Disagreement
The search for compromise: Philip of Hesse

The failure of compromise: the Marburg Colloquy

5 | Reasons Why Zwingli is Less Historically Significant than Luther

The beliefs and attitudes of Zwingli and Luther were very similar. However, Luther is regarded as one of the most significant characters of the sixteenth century, while Zwingli is hardly remembered outside his own country. Why is there this great difference?

Luther's survival

It is tempting to offer an explanation in terms of Zwingli's early death, which occurred just as he was reaching the peak of his influence. His reputation in Zurich was established, and the Marburg Colloquy had further enhanced his reputation in southern Germany. It could be argued that if Luther had died and Zwingli had survived, their roles might have been reversed. But this is unconvincing. The two men shared common beliefs and pursued similar policies, but Luther towered above Zwingli in many other respects.

Luther's charisma

Most obvious was the effect that Luther had on the people who met him. Because he was so clearly a man of charisma whom others could recognise as a superior being without losing face, men of distinction were prepared to act as his supporters and even as his disciples. This allowed Luther's ideas to be spread widely through the good will of local leaders who supported him. It also meant that many local leaders were prepared to trust his judgement in matters of disputed theology, so ensuring that the unified nature of the movement he had started was largely maintained. Zwingli did not have the same authority. Although he was respected as a man of great learning, he was never able to build up a band of devoted followers in the way that Luther did, and struggled to persuade even other cantons in the Swiss confederation to follow his teachings.

Key questions
Why is Luther considered to be of much greater historical importance than Zwingli? Which of the reasons given in this section do you find the most convincing?

Luther's popular appeal

Luther was also able to establish a dominant position in the minds of ordinary people throughout much of Germany. Whereas Zwingli and his followers produced a trickle of publications, Luther, all by himself, produced a flood. But the difference was not only one of quantity. It was also a matter of quality. Zwingli's writings were calm, clearly reasoned – and boring. In contrast, many of Luther's were couched in the rough and ready terms that appealed to the tastes and prejudices of the multitude. Luther's writings were eagerly sought, widely bought and rapidly passed from hand to hand. Zwingli's were not.

Luther's timing

Luther achieved fame several years before Zwingli, who was therefore always following in his shadow. Because their messages were so similar it was almost impossible for Zwingli to create a distinct impact in areas where Luther's work was already known. So he found much of his 'natural market' was already saturated.

Luther's location

Luther was also fortunate in the geographical position of Saxony, his adopted state. From his base in Wittenberg his message could radiate to the thickly populated areas of Germany to the north, east, west and south-west. This was an important factor at a time when a journey of a few kilometres could be a major undertaking, and when news spread by word of mouth and ideas were shared in printed material that was often distributed by people on foot. Zwingli shared none of these advantages. He lived in a remote and mountainous region on the very edge of the German-speaking world. For his message to gain more than local circulation time was required, time in which Lutheranism had established itself as the Protestant orthodoxy of northern and eastern Germany, and rival leaders had grown up in southern Germany. So Zwinglianism had little scope for expansion outside Switzerland.

Luther's supporters

Nor did Zwinglianism have the trained personnel for such an expansion. Luther's work was centred on the university in Wittenberg. Hundreds of young men were attracted to it from all parts of Germany and beyond. Many of them returned to their native areas after several years of study during which they had become convinced Lutherans, and acted very much as unpaid **missionaries**. It is possible to trace the spread of Luther's ideas partly in terms of returning students from the University of Wittenberg. There was no university in Zurich, and Zwingli was killed before he could establish an effective mechanism for training recruits to his faith. So he had no pool of potential missionaries.

Key term

Missionaries
People who attempt to convert others to a particular religious faith.

Zwingli was essentially one of the interesting 'might-have-beens' of sixteenth-century history. Like Luther, he was a magisterial reformer. In other words, he shared with Luther what many have seen as a typically Germanic insistence that change must come in carefully planned stages, without public disturbance, and be led by the city magistrates. He emphasised the need for discipline. As a result he led Zurich in a fundamental redirection of religious belief and practice which was achieved virtually without bloodshed or major discord.

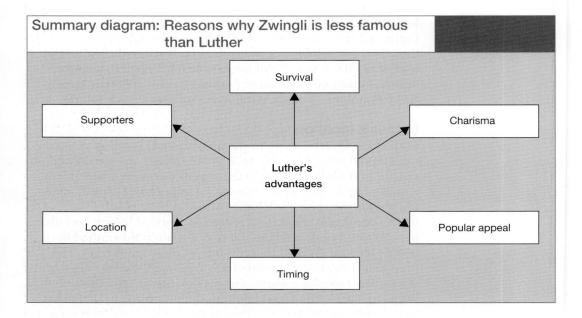

Summary diagram: Reasons why Zwingli is less famous than Luther

Study Guide: AS Questions

In the style of OCR B

Answer **both** parts of your chosen question.

(a) Explain the similarities and differences between the beliefs and attitudes of Zwingli and Luther.
[Explaining ideas, attitudes and beliefs]   (25 marks)

(b) How is the failure of the Colloquy of Marburg best explained?
[Explaining actions and circumstances]   (25 marks)

Exam tips

Remind yourself of the basics in the Exam tips in Chapter 2 (page 44).

(a) Your initial focus needs to explain the extent to which Luther and Zwingli agreed and differed in beliefs and in attitudes (distinguish between those two, considering also their different temperaments – as was illustrated so clearly at Marburg in 1529). You can initially point out that they shared much in common – crucially a Christianity built on justification by faith (*sola fide*) and the supremacy of Biblical authority (*sola scriptura*). You should also stress their common rejection of adult baptism. Then move on to consider core differences between them, notably the role to be played by reason in understanding the Bible, the theology of the Eucharist and the relationship of the Church to the political authorities (Luther came from territory governed by princes, whereas Zwingli's Switzerland was ruled by town councils). For Luther, Zwingli had twisted scripture. Given that unity between the evangelicals failed, it is the disagreements that really matter.

One issue not to miss out would be the question of how far Zwingli was influenced by Luther or whether he arrived at his core ideas independently. Scholars are still unsure what the truth is so note it but don't spend much time on it beyond stressing that Zwingli implemented reform independently of Luther. To put differences in context, you might devote most of this section to explanation of the significance of the bad relationship between Wittenberg and Zurich. 1529 was a time of crisis. Very few agreed with the 'Protest' made at the Diet of Speyer, and even fewer signed Philipp of Hesse's defensive military alliance. Agreement between Luther and Zwingli would have boosted morale and opened the way to a strong anti-Catholic bloc from the Upper Rhine to Switzerland. But the deep splits dividing the Protestant world could not be bridged and, in consequence, the military power of the Swiss was denied to the Lutherans should the emperor try to impose the 1521 Edict of Worms by force.

(b) The best way of approaching this question is to make notes under two headings: differing ideas and differing personalities. Given the wording of the question, you must also evaluate their relative importance so you answer directly 'best explained'.

Eucharistic theology may be the subject of your first column. Zwingli's view of the Eucharist was a variety of Protestantism more radical than Luther's (but all varieties were more radical than Luther's). To Zwingli, Luther had failed to purge the Eucharist of its Catholic notions – there could be no real presence (among the many evangelical leaders, an idea unique to Luther). Luther's position was based on a literal interpretation of the Biblical text, but where he took Jesus' words literally, Zwingli (and all the others) took it as figurative; by 'is', Jesus meant 'signifies'. To Luther that introduced an unnecessary complexity. A core part of your answer must be that Marburg failed over the question of whether there was a real presence or not.

The second column must focus on authority in the Reformation. Even early Protestantism involved a broad range of ideas and groupings. Luther and Zwingli were rival leaders (among others) in a very disunited collection of evangelical churches. Neither would compromise and the clash of personalities was impossible to miss (Luther banging the table and jabbing his finger). Both were proud men who had accomplished much. Each seems to have disliked the other. Philipp of Hesse and Melanchthon understood just how much these two needed to work together, but even cooperation proved impossible; unity was out of the question. Make sure you show you know that Zwingli and Luther agreed fourteen of the fifteen articles on the agenda. It is easy to blame short-tempered Luther, but in Augsburg in 1530 (when neither was present), discussions collapsed on the same subject. Marburg failed because of a clash of ideas (ideology, if you prefer). The humanist rationality of Zurich and the combative dogmatism of Luther were incompatible.

The Radical Reformation

POINTS TO CONSIDER

The dominant personality of the European Reformation was Martin Luther, followed a long way behind by Ulrich Zwingli. However, there were many other reformers in Europe, inspired by Luther's example and teachings, who championed their own particular forms of Christianity around the same time.

These reformers are collectively known as the Radicals. Just as 'Protestant' is a loose term used by historians to cover a number of groups such as the Lutherans and the Zwinglians, the term 'Radical' encompasses a wide range of disparate groups. These groups had little in common except the fact that their beliefs and practices were regarded by both Catholics and Protestants alike as dangerously extreme and subversive.

This chapter examines the Radical Reformation through the following themes:

- Reasons for the persecution of the Radicals
- Switzerland: Zwingli and the Swiss Brethren
- Germany: Luther and Thomas Müntzer
- Reasons why the Radicals were crushed so effectively
- Legacy of the Radical Reformation.

Key dates

1523	Switzerland: the Swiss Brethren argued against infant baptism in Zurich ('anabaptism')
1524	Germany: Thomas Müntzer took control of the Peasants' War and demanded a community of goods ('communitarianism')
1525	Switzerland: Swiss Brethren members were imprisoned and tortured
1525	Germany: Müntzerites were crushed at Frankenhausen by an alliance of Protestant and Catholic forces Müntzer was executed
1526	Conrad Grebel died in prison

	Felix Mantz was executed by drowning
1527	Remaining Radicals vainly attempt to unite forces in the Martyr's Synod and through the Schleitheim Articles
1528	Balthasar Hubmaier was burnt at the stake
1533	Melchior Hoffman was imprisoned by Bucer after claiming that Strasbourg was destined to be the 'New Jerusalem'
1535	Radical Melchiorites led by Jan Matthys and Jan Beukels of Leyden took control of Münster
1536	Radicals at Münster were crushed by an alliance of Protestant and Catholic forces

1 | Reasons for the Persecution of the Radicals

Key question
Why was the Radical movement persecuted so mercilessly?

The ferocity with which the Radicals were persecuted by Catholics and Protestants alike is difficult to understand. The 'Radical movement' was actually not particularly **radical**, and certainly never constituted anything vaguely approaching a centralised movement. And yet these same facts actually help to explain the level of persecution that the Radicals faced.

Weak organisation

Radicals
From the Latin word for 'root'. A point of view which is regarded as being extreme and outlandish.

Key term

Firstly the Radicals were not united in their beliefs or under a single leader. 'Radicals' is a general term covering a bewildering confusion of groups with such names as Huttites, Hutterites, Münsterites, Müntzerites, Mennonites and Melchiorites. As a result they were unable to resist their persecutors effectively.

Secondly, Luther's revolt had turned Europe into two armed camps: Catholics and Lutherans. Religious faith was no longer a private matter but one of state security. The papacy by this time had become a separate state, in which the Protestant princes were all-powerful within their territories. Radical sects were therefore prime targets for persecution – not strictly because they were radical, but simply because they did not fit in. Whether they found themselves in Catholic or Lutheran territory, they were regarded as 'the enemy within'.

Controversial beliefs

The Radicals regarded the Reformation as unfinished business. In their view, Luther and other magisterial reformers were too weak or emotionally attached to the Catholic faith to follow the Reformation through to its logical conclusions. The Radicals rejected the idea that half-measures and compromises were necessary to avoid social and political chaos and pursued reforms from which Luther and Zwingli were at pains to disassociate themselves:

- 'Iconoclasts' agreed with Luther that images of saints in churches were a distraction from worship, but went much further by violently stripping them out in a process approaching vandalism.
- 'Anabaptists' rejected infant baptism because it was not found in the Bible; but without infant baptism it was feared that a whole generation could grow up uncontrolled by the Church and state.
- 'Communitarians' campaigned for a redistribution of the wealth and power of the rich to the poor, arguing that Luther's idea of a 'priesthood of all believers' meant that inequalities between people were sinful.

Such outlandish ideas threatened to destroy the fabric of society. Eager to distance themselves from their 'misguided' disciples, the magisterial reformers themselves encouraged the rulers of Europe to crush them without mercy. This process can be seen in Switzerland, where Zwingli attacked the Swiss Brethren, and in Germany, where Luther attacked the followers of Thomas Müntzer.

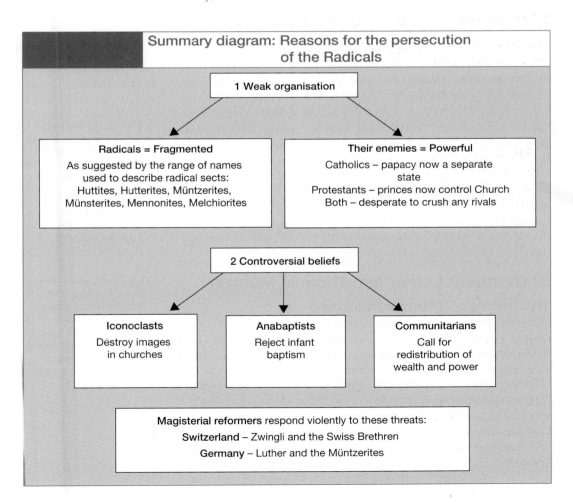

Summary diagram: Reasons for the persecution of the Radicals

1 Weak organisation

Radicals = Fragmented
As suggested by the range of names used to describe radical sects: Huttites, Hutterites, Müntzerites, Münsterites, Mennonites, Melchiorites

Their enemies = Powerful
Catholics – papacy now a separate state
Protestants – princes now control Church
Both – desperate to crush any rivals

2 Controversial beliefs

Iconoclasts
Destroy images in churches

Anabaptists
Reject infant baptism

Communitarians
Call for redistribution of wealth and power

Magisterial reformers respond violently to these threats:
Switzerland – Zwingli and the Swiss Brethren
Germany – Luther and the Müntzerites

2 | Switzerland: Zwingli and the Swiss Brethren

The beliefs of the Swiss Brethren

Geographically, the Radicals can be traced to Switzerland. Zwingli's simplification of the Eucharist as a commemorative service and his willingness to debate the validity of infant baptism encouraged the growth of radical ideas. In 1523, the **Swiss Brethren** – Balthasar Hubmaier, Felix Mantz and Conrad Grebel – used Luther's ideas of *sola scriptura* to argue that baptism for infants had no Biblical basis and so it should be restricted to informed adults. Their first baptism was of a man named George Blaurock the same year.

The actions of the authorities against the Swiss Brethren

These anabaptist views challenged the foundations on which Christian society was based. The act of baptism transformed people not only into Christians, but also into members of the state. When the Brethren then rejected the compulsory military service and the swearing of oaths of loyalty, it suggested that they were anarchists.

In contrast to the Radicals, magisterial reformers like Zwingli and Luther had accepted the role of the state (princes, city councils, magistrates) in organising religious activity if the Church was to be reformed safely. So Zurich acted swiftly and decisively against the Swiss Brethren. In 1525 Grebel, Mantz and Blaurock were imprisoned; Hubmaier was subjected to torture and banishment. The following year the Zurich Council declared that the Brethren should be executed 'without mercy'; with cruel irony they stipulated that the Brethren's commitment to baptism meant that the method to be used should be drowning. Grebel had already died of natural causes by this point, but Mantz was swiftly plunged into a watery grave whilst Blaurock – a non-citizen – was beaten through the streets and expelled. In 1528 Hubmaier was hunted down and arrested by the imperial government. It was decided to burn him at the stake, while his wife was thrown into the River Danube with a boulder round her neck.

3 | Germany: Luther and Thomas Müntzer

The beliefs of Thomas Müntzer

While the Swiss Brethren were causing trouble for Zwingli, a priest named Thomas Müntzer was causing problems for Martin Luther in the city of Zwickau in Germany. Müntzer was an iconoclast and a communitarian. Even more alarmingly for the evangelical reformers, he was a **spiritualist**, arguing that God communicated directly with the believer and that the Bible was a 'paper Pope' which obscured God's message. Müntzer became convinced that God was telling him that the **Second Coming** of Christ was at hand and that it was the duty of the godly to take up arms against their enemies.

Key questions
What radical groups operated inside Switzerland, and how were they dealt with? What were the main beliefs of the Swiss Brethren?

Key terms

Swiss Brethren
A group of radical reformers based in Zwingli's Zurich who argued that only adults could be baptised. Sometimes known as 'Anabaptists'.

Spiritualists
A group of extreme Protestants who rejected the Bible in favour of direct communication with God through prayer.

Key dates

The Swiss Brethren argued against infant baptism in Zurich ('anabaptism'). Condemned by Zwingli: 1523

Swiss Brethren members were imprisoned and tortured: 1525

Key questions
What radical groups operated inside Germany, and how were they dealt with? Why was Thomas Müntzer considered such a threat?

Like the Swiss Brethren, Müntzer refused to see the distinction between religion, society and politics. Luther was determined to keep religious and secular affairs separate (referring to them as 'the two kingdoms'). However, Müntzer argued that the 'priesthood of all believers' meant that all men were equal; therefore the princes had no right to dictate the faith or social arrangements of the peasants. For Müntzer, a reformation of religion needed to be matched by a reformation of society and politics.

A banknote from communist East Germany depicting Thomas Müntzer. Müntzer's leadership of the peasants earned him a reputation as a hero of the common people.

The Peasants' War and the death of Müntzer

Luther bitterly attacked Müntzer and his followers in a series of sermons and persuaded the authorities to expel the '**Zwickau Prophets**' from the city. Müntzer, denouncing Luther as 'Doctor Liar', headed into south Germany to take advantage of growing peasant discontent. When the Peasants' War broke out in 1524, Müntzer's charisma and energy propelled him into the leadership of the movement.

Whilst travelling through Thuringia on his way back to Wittenberg in May 1525, Luther was booed and spat on by groups of peasants. Shortly afterwards he wrote the notorious pamphlet, *Against the Murderous, Thieving Hordes of Peasants*. In it, he encouraged the princes to 'smite, stab and strangle' the rebels, whose souls belonged to the devil 'for all eternity'.

Müntzer hastily gathered a force of 8000 men at Frankenhausen, where he awaited the armies of several princes marching against the city. Prior to the battle, Müntzer was inspired by the appearance of a glorious rainbow in the sky and delivered an impassioned speech to his followers claiming that God would enable them to catch the bullets of their opponents in their sleeves. Müntzer's hot-line to God was faulty; 5000 peasants were slaughtered in the ensuing conflict. Müntzer himself was captured, brutally tortured, and then beheaded after being forced to make a humiliating apology for his 'misguided' actions. The Peasants' War was over.

Profile: Thomas Müntzer (c.1489–1525)

c.1489	– Müntzer was born in Thuringia, central Germany. As a young man he studied for the priesthood, becoming fluent in Greek, Latin and Hebrew
1513	– Ordained as a priest and took up his first parish post
1517–19	– Stayed in Wittenberg and supported Martin Luther in the Indulgences Controversy
1520	– Became a priest in Zwickau, Saxony. He was persuaded by the 'Zwickau Prophets' to reject infant baptism (anabaptism)
1521	– Expelled from Zwickau by the city authorities for his radical views
1523	– Took up a post in Allstedt, Saxony, and married a former nun
1524	– Expelled from Allstedt after claiming that God communicated with him directly through dreams (spiritualism)
1524	– Expelled from Mühlhausen, Thuringia, after claiming that Luther's 'priesthood of all believers' meant that the rich should share their wealth with the poor (communitarianism)
1525	– Became a leader of the Peasants' War and told his followers that God would protect them from harm
1525	– The Battle of Frankenhausen: Catholic and Protestant forces crushed the Peasants' War. Müntzer was tortured then executed

Thomas Müntzer, like many radicals, started off a loyal disciple of Martin Luther but quickly became frustrated with what he saw as Luther's refusal to follow his ideas through properly. He agreed with Luther that the sale of indulgences by the Catholic Church was sinful. He agreed too that faith, not 'good works', was essential to get into heaven. He also agreed that a Bible in the language of the people was necessary to let people discover their faith for themselves.

However, to Luther's alarm, Müntzer refused to stop there. Instead, he took Luther's idea of *sola scriptura* and used it to reach an 'Anabaptist' position – the idea that child baptism should be rejected altogether. Müntzer argued that there were no examples of children being baptised in the Bible; therefore, God only wants adults – making an informed choice – to be members of his Church. From this point, Luther regarded Müntzer as a rebel. This impression was confirmed when Müntzer adopted a 'spiritualist' position, claiming that God could communicate directly with the believer through visions and dreams, not just through the Holy Bible as Luther argued. Müntzer's final heresy was to adopt a 'communitarian' position – the idea that the rich should be forced to share their wealth and power with the poor. He reasoned that Luther's idea of a 'priesthood of all believers' meant that all men were equal in the eyes of God, so any inequalities that existed between them on earth were the work of the devil.

In conclusion, Müntzer refused to accept Luther's view that the Reformation should be controlled by moderate middle-ranking magistrates. He also rejected the idea that a Reformation of the Church did not require drastic changes in society and politics. Instead, he argued that Luther should accept that the Reformation he had started meant the rejection not just of papal power but also the oppressive social and political structures that had been built around it. This made Müntzer a natural leader of the Peasants' War. Luther reacted violently, fully supporting the slaughter of the rebels at the Battle of Frankenhausen in 1525 – and in the process destroying his reputation as a hero of the common man.

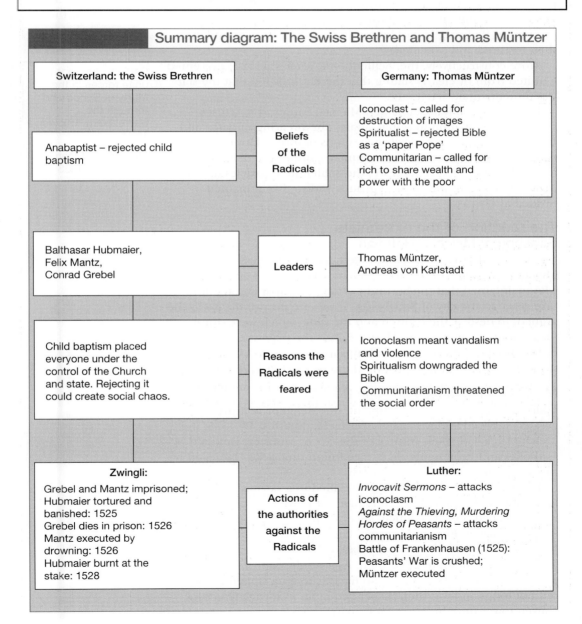

Summary diagram: The Swiss Brethren and Thomas Müntzer

Switzerland: the Swiss Brethren — **Germany: Thomas Müntzer**

Beliefs of the Radicals	
Anabaptist – rejected child baptism	Iconoclast – called for destruction of images Spiritualist – rejected Bible as a 'paper Pope' Communitarian – called for rich to share wealth and power with the poor

Leaders	
Balthasar Hubmaier, Felix Mantz, Conrad Grebel	Thomas Müntzer, Andreas von Karlstadt

Reasons the Radicals were feared	
Child baptism placed everyone under the control of the Church and state. Rejecting it could create social chaos.	Iconoclasm meant vandalism and violence Spiritualism downgraded the Bible Communitarianism threatened the social order

Actions of the authorities against the Radicals	
Zwingli: Grebel and Mantz imprisoned; Hubmaier tortured and banished: 1525 Grebel dies in prison: 1526 Mantz executed by drowning: 1526 Hubmaier burnt at the stake: 1528	**Luther:** *Invocavit Sermons* – attacks iconoclasm *Against the Thieving, Murdering Hordes of Peasants* – attacks communitarianism Battle of Frankenhausen (1525): Peasants' War is crushed; Müntzer executed

4 | Reasons Why the Radicals were Crushed so Effectively

Key question
Why was the persecution of the Radicals so effective?

Persecution of a minority often has the result in driving them underground in the short term, only to see them resurge later on with greater resolve and unity. However, the Radicals never recovered from the defeat of the peasants at the Battle of Frankenhausen.

The reaction of the moderates

A meeting between leading Radicals was organised in 1527, but this 'Martyr's Synod' was more concerned with celebrating their persecution as proof of their divine mission than formulating means of avoiding it in the future (in fact, one of the most prominent Radicals, Hans Hut, was arrested whilst in attendance, then tortured and executed).

Martyr
Someone who dies in defence of their religious beliefs.

More constructively, the 'Schleitheim Articles' (1527) presented a united front by clearly stating that the Radicals felt that the state was fundamentally irrelevant.

Radicals attempt to unite forces in the Martyr's Synod and through the Schleitheim Articles: 1527

Melchior Hoffman imprisoned: 1533

Drawn up by a Radical named Michael Sattler, the Articles rejected participation in public affairs, the swearing of oaths and the use of 'unchristian, devilish weapons of force'. However, controversial issues such as communitarianism were deliberately ignored, not tackled. Therefore, the Schleitheim Articles did not really unite the various radical groups and so they remained divided and weak.

The reaction of the extremists
Strasbourg: Melchior Hoffman

The most influential of the extreme radical groups were the Melchiorites. They were led by Melchior Hoffman, a spiritualist who maintained that the Second Coming of Christ was about to take place in the city of Strasbourg. It was the duty of the godly, he argued, to destroy the Church and the state, which were sinful instruments of oppression. Martin Bucer, the magisterial reformer in Strasbourg, did not agree with this interpretation of events and swiftly threw Hoffman in prison, where he died in 1543.

Münster: Jan Matthys and Jan Beukels

Following Hoffman's imprisonment, the Melchiorite movement he created survived and was taken over by Jan Matthys. By 1535, the Melchiorites had taken control of the city of Münster. Detested by Catholics and Protestants alike, they found themselves besieged by their opponents almost immediately.

When, in April 1535, Matthys was killed in a skirmish, leadership was assumed by Jan Beukels of Leyden, a former tailor who abolished the city council, legalised polygamy, and had himself crowned King of Münster. The Melchiorites held out until June of 1536, when the city capitulated to its enemies and its leaders were gruesomely executed. As a result, radical leaders were persecuted mercilessly. 'King' Jan had his tongue ripped out with red hot tongs and was then suspended in an iron cage from the church tower until his corpse fell apart.

Radical Melchiorites led by Jan Matthys and Jan Beukels of Leyden took control of Münster: 1535

Radicals at Münster were crushed by an alliance of Protestant and Catholic forces: 1536

Some historians have sought to diminish the insanity of the Münster experiment. Firstly, they argue that although 'sins' such as complaining became punishable by death, this was just a desperate attempt to maintain control in a city under attack. Secondly, although polygamy was encouraged, they insist that this was just a practical reaction to the fact that women outnumbered men four to one. However, these arguments overlook the fact that Jan Beukels was clearly insane – a man who beheaded one of his 16 wives for nagging and then furiously trampled on the corpse; a man who crowned himself king of the world in a lavish ceremony at the very moment that enemy forces were battering the city into submission.

The steeple of St Lambert's cathedral in Münster. The bodies of Jan of Leyden and two other Anabaptists were placed in these cages after they were tortured and killed. Why did Catholics and Protestants deal so ferociously with the Radicals?

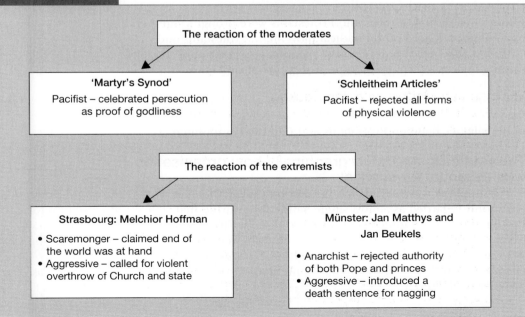

Summary diagram: Reasons why the persecution of the Radicals was so effective

The reaction of the moderates

'Martyr's Synod'
Pacifist – celebrated persecution as proof of godliness

'Schleitheim Articles'
Pacifist – rejected all forms of physical violence

The reaction of the extremists

Strasbourg: Melchior Hoffman
- Scaremonger – claimed end of the world was at hand
- Aggressive – called for violent overthrow of Church and state

Münster: Jan Matthys and Jan Beukels
- Anarchist – rejected authority of both Pope and princes
- Aggressive – introduced a death sentence for nagging

5 | Legacy of the Radical Reformation

Key question
What was the legacy of the Radical Reformation?

The convenient answer is to say that the Radicals in Europe were ultimately of no real significance, although some of them ultimately drifted to and flourished in the New World. However, this is a rather simple interpretation.

It is true that in the USA there are, to this day, flourishing communities not only of Hutterites, but also of Mennonites. These peace-loving people live by the ideas of Menno Simons, who had rallied the remaining Radicals after Münster with his sublime *Foundation of Christian Doctrine* and is widely regarded as the most successful and influential of all the Radicals.

It is also true that in Europe the Radicals became even more divided after the Münster debacle and unable to make a direct impact. Spiritualists such as Caspar Schwenkfeld, Hans Denck and Sebastian Franck muddied the waters even further by rejecting the Bible ('the paper Pope') in favour of divine inspiration. This entailed the rejection of all established forms of religion, which was fatal given the fact that the exploits of 'King' Jan Beukels had hardened opinion against the Radicals. In the words of the Protestant magisterial reformer Bullinger, 'God opened the eyes of the governments by the revolt of Münster, and thereafter no one would trust even those Anabaptists who claimed to be innocent.'

Nevertheless, to dismiss the Radicals because they were crushed is to miss the point. History is not just about 'winners' – if that were the case, historians would hardly bother to study Adolf Hitler. The impact that the Radicals had on Europe was not that which they were hoping for, but that does not diminish the scale of their importance, which is outlined below.

The Radicals clarified the battle lines between Protestants and Catholics

In the short term, Catholics and Protestants were brought together by a common hatred of the Radical movement. Protestants and Catholics alike produced a flood of pamphlets and sermons making it clear – from their respective points of view – why the Radicals had got it wrong. In the long term, however, these pronouncements merely served to clarify the battle lines between the two groups. Once the Radicals had been defeated, the purpose of the alliance between Protestants and Catholics evaporated.

The Radicals illustrated graphically how organisation was essential for survival

The example of the Radicals was not lost on **Calvin**, the man commonly regarded as almost single-handedly ensuring that Protestantism had a long-term future throughout Europe and beyond. Organisation and unity, thought Calvin, were essential for survival, a matter he made clear through his *Ecclesiastical Ordinances* which laid down a detailed, methodical structure for the reformed church.

Calvin
A second-generation Protestant reformer based in Geneva who focused on issues of organisation as much as belief.

Key figure

The Radicals destroyed the credibility of the Lutheran Reformation as a 'people's movement'

When Luther produced his *Ninety-five Theses* against Church abuses – and then proceeded to stand up against the might of the Pope and the Holy Roman Emperor – he became something of a folk hero. In fact, Luther was far from being a champion of the common man's right to think for himself. He was deeply suspicious of the demands of the ordinary people and incapable of listening to anybody who dared to disagree with his views. This was proven beyond doubt by his handling of the Radicals. Rather than accept that their relationship with God was just as valid as his own, he instead promoted mass murder of those people who had dared to take his ideas further than he had intended.

The Radicals did not kill off the supposed '**liberalism**' of the Reformation; they merely highlighted that it had never really been liberal in the first place. In the words of the Catholic priest and historian Johann von Döllinger, writing in the nineteenth century:

> Historically nothing is more incorrect than the assertion that the Reformation was a movement in favour of intellectual freedom. The exact contrary is the truth. For themselves, it is true, Lutherans and Calvinists claimed liberty of conscience … but to grant it to others never occurred to them so long as they were the stronger side. The complete extirpation of … everything that stood in their way was regarded by the reformers as something entirely natural.

The Protestants, no less than the Catholics, preached tolerance only when it suited them, just as the Radicals were perfectly prepared to use violence when they felt it would be to their advantage. Sadly, it seems, tolerance is almost always preached by the downtrodden rather than the powerful, and out of necessity rather than genuine conviction.

The key debate

Up until relatively recent times, the Radical Reformation was dismissed as a lunatic fringe movement of marginal interest and little importance. Martin Luther dismissed the Radicals as '*Schwärmer*' (fanatics) and this set the general tone for studies until the mid-twentieth century. The Radicals were almost universally dismissed as theologically ignorant, personally perverse and mentally imbalanced, with only the occasional historian such as Ernst Troeltsch striking a more sympathetic note.

This consensus changed following the publication of *The Anabaptist Vision* by the American Mennonite Harold Bender in 1944. His view, later developed by George H. Williams in *The Radical Reformation* (1972), was that the Radicals were the most principled of the reform movements that emerged following Luther's revolt. Bender argued that the Radicals were peace-loving people who had grown out of the Swiss Brethren movement in Zwingli's Zurich. They stayed true to the idea that all people were

---

Key term

Liberalism
A political philosophy that champions individual freedoms and personal rights.

equal in the eyes of God and believed that this necessitated major social reforms, unlike Luther who lost his nerve and sided instead with the ruling classes against the ordinary people during the Peasants' War of 1524–25. Far from being crushed, they flourished in the United States. In his words, 'The great principles of freedom of conscience [and] separation of church and state ... so essential to democracy, ultimately are derived from the Anabaptists of the Reformation period.'

Bender's view of the Radicals as enlightened social revolutionaries was shared by the communist historians of East Germany who presented them as the vanguard of the 'People's Reformation' (M.M. Smirin) and the 'early bourgeois revolution in Germany' (Max Steinmetz). Between the defeat of Müntzer's peasants in 1525 and the suppression of Jan Beukel's kingdom in Münster, it was argued that the Radical reformers preserved the spirit of the Popular Reformation against the conservative magistrates.

However, this sympathetic treatment of the Radicals was challenged in the 1970s. Claus-Peter Clasen attacked the communist idea that the Radicals were social reformers by suggesting that they established no clear link with the peasant rebels in 1524–25. James M. Sayer argued that Bender's view of the Radicals as harmless pacifists had only been possible by conveniently ignoring those groups and individuals (such as the Melchiorites and Thomas Müntzer) who called for the violent overthrow of their enemies. Sayer developed this argument in collaboration with Werner O. Packull and Klaus Deppermann, who together identified three major strands to the Radical movement: the Swiss Brethren, the German Anabaptists and the Dutch Melchiorites. It was on this basis that the term 'Anabaptist' was considered no longer appropriate as a general term of reference, and since this time historians have preferred to use the broader term 'Radical' to cover the various strands that made up the movement.

Some key books in the debate:

Harold S. Bender, *The Anabaptist Vision*, Scottdale (Herald Press, 1944)

Geoffrey Dipple, *Just As in the Time of the Apostles: Uses of History in the Radical Reformation* (Pandora Press, 2005)

George H. Williams, *The Radical Reformation*, reprint of 1962 version (Truman State University Press, 2001)

A woodcut depicting Luther as the devil's bagpipe. How was Luther's reputation affected by his handling of the Radical reformers?

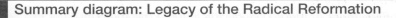

Summary diagram: Legacy of the Radical Reformation

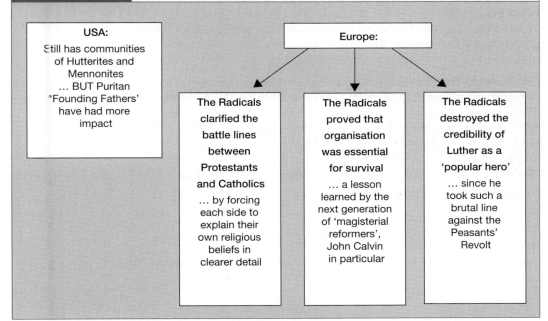

USA:

Still has communities of Hutterites and Mennonites … BUT Puritan 'Founding Fathers' have had more impact

Europe:

The Radicals clarified the battle lines between Protestants and Catholics
… by forcing each side to explain their own religious beliefs in clearer detail

The Radicals proved that organisation was essential for survival
… a lesson learned by the next generation of 'magisterial reformers', John Calvin in particular

The Radicals destroyed the credibility of Luther as a 'popular hero'
… since he took such a brutal line against the Peasants' Revolt

Study Guide: AS Questions
In the style of OCR A

Study the five sources on **Luther and the Radicals**, and then answer **both** sub-questions. It is recommended that you spend two-thirds of your time in answering part **(b)**.

(a) Study Sources A and D.
Compare these sources as evidence for Luther's beliefs in the authority of the Bible. (30 marks)

(b) Study all the sources.
Use your own knowledge to assess how far the sources support the interpretation that Luther was mainly responsible for the failure to resolve religious disputes between Protestants in the 1520s. (70 marks)

Luther and the Radicals

Source A
Martin Luther, letter to Philipp Melanchthon, 1522
Luther writes to a close friend about his suspicions of a radical Protestant group:

I do not approve of your moderation towards these radicals. We should not immediately accept their views but test them out from the Bible. You should enquire about their spiritual condition. Do not approve of them simply because they are said to be pleasant, quiet and devout. I always expected the Devil to be at work and thought he would not do it through Papists. The Devil is stirring up this grievous division among our followers and us, but God will quickly trample him under our feet.

Source B
Erasmus, letter to Martin Bucer, the leading religious reformer in Strasbourg, 1527
The leading Catholic humanist blames Luther in particular for the arguments about religion that Luther had with other religious reformers:

I deplore the constant in-fighting between religious leaders. Apart from the Zwickau Prophets and the Anabaptists, just look at the spiteful pamphlets written by Luther and Zwingli against each other. I have always condemned the venom of such religious leaders and their followers encourage them. They should have set an example of godly and patient conduct, which would have made God's truth widely acceptable. Did Luther not realise how foolish he looked? This is the movement's leader!

Source C
The Colloquy of Marburg, October 1529
An eye-witness report of opening statements at a meeting between Luther and other leading reformers to resolve religious disputes between Protestants. The meeting was organised by Count Philip of Hesse:

Friege, the Chancellor of Hesse: My gracious Prince, Philip of Hesse, has called you to this meeting in order to settle the quarrel about the Lord's Supper. Much depends on it. My Prince wishes that everybody should seek God's honour, not his own advantage, in a spirit of brotherly friendship. Both parties should present their arguments with moderation.

Luther: Illustrious Prince! I do not doubt that this meeting has been planned with good intentions. I agreed to come when Philip made preparations for it. I felt that I had to obey the wishes of this most excellent ruler. But I do not want to change my view, which is as firm as a rock.

Source D

The Colloquy of Marburg, October 1529
Leading reformers debate aspects of the Bible at Marburg:

Luther (on the concept of consubstantiation, i.e. Luther's 'Iron in the Fire' theory): I repeat again that I do not accept mathematical dimensions as applicable to Holy Scripture, because God is greater than all the mathematicians.

Oecolampadius: Where, doctor, does it say in the Bible that we should close our eyes to its meaning?

Luther: If we debated for a century it would make no difference. Show me the text and I will be satisfied. We must not interpret in our own way the words of our Lord.

Source E

R.W. Scribner, The German Reformation*, 1986*
A modern historian comments on a leading radical:

Müntzer was driven by a radical apocalyptic vision, believing that the end of the world was imminent, and that the rule of God's elect, the Saints, would usher it in. In Müntzer's vision, this would rectify many of the glaring injustices suffered by Christians in the world. Initially he demanded with prophetic fervour that the Princes should step in to further reform, to hasten the rule of the Saints. Here he was doing no more, although with more prophetic passion, than Luther had done in his 1520 *Address to the Christian Nobility*. However, Müntzer quickly went a step further, threatening the Princes that if they did not fulfil their Christian duty, they would suffer the wrath of God, and that the task of rooting out the ungodly would be taken up by the Saints themselves.

Exam tips

(a) In a comparison of two sources, you must make direct references to the sources themselves, identify any features that are complementary as well as contradictory, and comment on the nature of the sources' authenticity, completeness, consistency, typicality and usefulness. You are not expected to consider all of these qualities but to discuss the most important. Remember that you should only use your own knowledge to provide a context for the sources and your answer should not be driven by contextual knowledge. Some of the main points you might discuss are:

- Both Sources A and D confirm that the Bible was fundamental to Luther's beliefs.
- Luther remained constant in his distrust of radicals. Source A was written privately and before the Radicals had fully developed their views; Source D was stated publicly and after the full effects of radical groups had become apparent to Luther.
- Luther in both sources reveals his own self-confidence that borders on hypocrisy. He declares that the Bible should be the source of knowledge and that no one should try to interpret the words, but that is precisely what he had done.

(b) The answer requires a good balance between your own knowledge and an analysis of all five sources. Your answer might consider some of the following points:

- The sources mainly hold Luther responsible but other reformers contributed to the disharmony among Protestants.
- Sources A, C and D suggest that Luther was unwilling to compromise because he believed he was right. Source A states that Luther was opposed to toleration although this was normal in the early sixteenth century; Source C shows Luther's intolerance even before the Marburg debate began, although the eye-witness may have been prejudiced against him; Source D shows that Luther's fundamentalist view of the Bible was bound to cause difficulties.
- Erasmus in Source B blames Luther and Zwingli (as well as other radicals) for their literary war – he too by 1527 had been a victim of Luther's pen which may have coloured his views.
- Source E blames Müntzer rather than Luther for peasant radicalism, though Luther does not entirely escape criticism.

In the style of OCR B

Answer **both** parts of your chosen question.

(a) How is Luther's quarrel with the Zwickau Prophets best explained?
[Explaining motives, actions and circumstances]   (25 marks)

(b) What was it about the Anabaptists that made them so persecuted?
[Explaining ideas, attitudes and beliefs]   (25 marks)

Exam tips

Re-read the general introduction in the Exam tips in Chapter 2 (page 44).

(a) You could start the essay looking at the issue from Luther's perspective or from that of Müntzer. Either way, you are dealing here with a clash of personalities as well as of ideas, and comparison will be essential to your explanation. Luther was a conservative, always anxious to keep things under control. He moved slowly. By contrast, Müntzer had the enthusiasm of the convert – having discovered the new truth, he rushed forward regardless. You could then consider how Luther's position and authority was being challenged. He had been left behind while hiding in the Wartburg. Meanwhile, in Zwickau women were preaching and adults were being re-baptised. Luther accused the Prophets of fanaticism, but Rome had levelled the same accusation at Luther himself.

Your next paragraphs need to focus on issues. For Müntzer it was all about ideas, but for Luther it was a matter of order and discipline – two sides of the Reformation that were often in tension. That an ill-educated blacksmith could be a religious leader might be fully logical under the priesthood of all believers, but non-professionals in charge was a step too far for Luther (women leaders were even less acceptable to him). The Wittenberg Movement shows that, almost from the start, there were alternative reformations.

Finally, consider rival concepts of organisation. Luther's top-down reformation was allied to the state and demanded the membership of all citizens. The Prophets, however, stood apart from the state and invited consenting adults to join them (hence adult baptism). This was the first case of the 'Magisterial Reformation' *v* the 'Radical Reformation', but it was not the last. When papal authority was rejected, who was to decide which interpretation was correct?

(b) The opening sections of this chapter give you an excellent framework for answering this question. Start by considering their weak organization: show that they were not one single group (e.g. Mennonites and Melchiorites, Hutterites and Huttites, Müntzerites and Münsterites) and were themselves divided over issues, e.g. polygamy – but contemporaries were too scared to notice such realities. Show also that their numbers were tiny – so did the authorities react out of all proportion to the reality of any 'threat'? The fact that they did shows how nervous princes and magistrates were of any dissent – the general turbulence of the reformation had put everyone on edge (especially after the Peasants' War).

You could then consider the next theme dealt with in this chapter – the controversial beliefs of the Radicals. Examine elements of Radical beliefs that jarred in sixteenth-century Europe, e.g. the more 'tabloid' issues like iconoclasm, polygamy, anabaptism and communitarianism. Note that Radicals were persecuted by Protestants as much as by Catholics, but focus on reasons why such ideas and practices alarmed contemporaries: they challenged deeply established social and economic patterns; they turned the world upside down, appearing to pull down the basic pillars of organised society – they threatened not religious reform but the destruction of society as it was understood.

You could then develop your answer with a detailed case study – 'King' Jan and the Münster experiment of 1534–35 – which united Catholic and Lutheran princes in the action to crush it. To sharpen your explanation, you could compare it to that other great popular uprising of the German Reformation, the Peasants' War. Both challenged social, economic and political norms of their day, but there was one core difference: the kingdom in Münster challenged the entire system of political power and every rule.

7 The Politics of Lutheranism

POINTS TO CONSIDER

When Luther disappeared from public view in May 1521, the future of Lutheranism was in grave doubt. Luther had been outlawed by the Emperor and excommunicated by the Church. His followers were disunited and still aimed at the reform of the existing Church rather than setting up a rival organisation. On the other side, the Catholics were led in Germany by an Emperor who was determined to reach a compromise with the Lutherans, or failing that to crush them by military force. Despite this, by 1555 Lutheranism had become so well established throughout Germany that Charles V was forced to recognise that the division in the Church was permanent. How was Lutheranism able to survive and thrive against such odds? Does the explanation lie in the actions of particular individuals, or deeper factors?

This chapter will seek to address these issues in the following manner:

- The spread of Lutheranism across Germany, 1522–30
- Explanations for the spread of Lutheranism, 1522–30
- Compromise fails, 1522–30
- Protestantism on the offensive, 1531–40
- Catholicism on the offensive, 1541–47
- Compromise succeeds, 1548–55.

Key dates

1521	Luther went into hiding after he was outlawed by the Edict of Worms
1522–29	Emperor Charles V was out of Germany
1525	Albrecht of Hohenzollern was converted to Lutheranism
1526	Philip of Hesse was converted to Lutheranism
1527	John, Elector of Saxony, was converted to Lutheranism
1529	Diet of Speyer: Lutherans 'protested' at the suggestion that the Edict of Worms be enforced

1530	Augsburg Confession: Lutherans drew up a common statement of belief for the first time
1531	League of Schmalkalden: Lutherans organised a military alliance
1534	Württemberg became Protestant
1535	Joachim, Elector of Brandenburg, became Protestant
1539	Heinrich, Duke of Saxony, became Protestant
1540	Philip of Hesse's reputation was destroyed by a bigamy scandal
1541	Diet of Regensburg: Charles V decided that military force was needed to crush the Lutherans
1544	The Ottoman Empire scaled down its European military campaigns
	Charles V turned his attention back to the Protestant problem
1547	Battle of Mühlberg: Charles V defeated the League of Schmalkalden
1548	Interim of Augsburg
1555	Peace of Augsburg: Charles V accepted that the religious divisions in the Empire are permanent

1 | The Spread of Lutheranism across Germany, 1522–30

The pattern of reform

There was a general pattern to reform that became common throughout the towns and cities of Germany which decided to adopt Luther's teachings. A small group of reformers, often led by a priest who had read many of Luther's writings, would attempt to persuade the general population that changes should be introduced. This was often done through public sermons.

Priests and scholars were often won over by Luther's theological publications which, for many, provided convincing answers to problems of belief that had long troubled them. To the lay people from all levels of society, who regarded him in some sense as a hero, his appeal was often that he challenged the abuses within the Church. He offered the prospect of relief from the financial demands of greedy priests locally, and of the Pope nationally. The process sometimes took place with the agreement of the local rulers, in some cases because they feared riots if they tried to prevent it.

Wherever enough local support could be gained for a change in practices (be it the removal of images from churches, the closure of monasteries, or some other matter), action was taken. The reformers would rarely agree among themselves on matters of

Key questions
What was the process by which Lutheranism became accepted in a local area? Why was it that this process, once started, was rarely stopped?

detail, and would often refer their disputes to Luther for settlement. Even then there would often be some who refused to abide by the verdict, and who would choose to move on to another town. In this way reforming ideas would be brought to places that knew little of them, and the process would continue.

The example of Wittenberg

In hundreds of towns and villages in all parts of Germany an unofficial Reformation of this type was begun. It was uncoordinated and very variable in outcome. In Wittenberg this all happened in 1521–22 while Luther was in Wartburg Castle. Churches were cleansed of images; the mass was performed partly in German, with the congregation receiving the wine as well as the bread; priests married; monks were persuaded to abandon their vows and to leave their monasteries; and riot was used to intimidate those who objected.

Frederick attempted to slow things down by forbidding further change until general agreement had been gained. However, the reformers largely ignored him, and the town council took it upon itself to overrule the Elector and to invite Luther to return to Wittenberg. This he willingly did, although he understood that Frederick would do nothing to protect him were he to be arrested by anyone loyal to the Emperor.

Luther's personal influence was such that he soon persuaded most of the town's leading citizens that change must come much more slowly, and only when its need was widely accepted. At this, some of the most active reformers left the town to seek a more sympathetic environment elsewhere. Among their number was Andreas Karlstadt, one of Luther's fellow professors at the university and one of his earliest supporters.

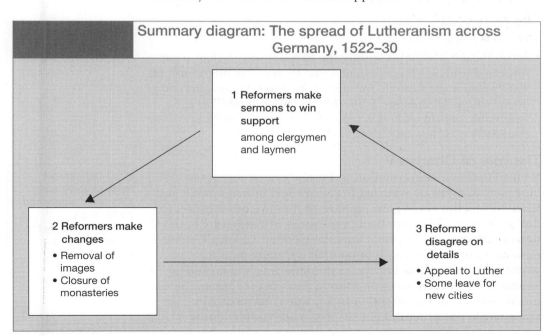

Summary diagram: The spread of Lutheranism across Germany, 1522–30

1 Reformers make sermons to win support
among clergymen and laymen

2 Reformers make changes
- Removal of images
- Closure of monasteries

3 Reformers disagree on details
- Appeal to Luther
- Some leave for new cities

2 | Explanations for the Spread of Lutheranism, 1522–30

By the mid-1520s it would have been necessary to execute tens of thousands of Protestants to crush the movement. But, although this would have been difficult, it would not have been impossible, as had been shown in earlier centuries when widespread heresy had been exterminated by massacring whole populations. A similar approach was adopted in Germany itself in 1525 at the end of the Peasants' War. How, then, was this random and disorganised collection of reformed communities able to maintain itself in the face of the hostility of the Emperor?

The role of Frederick the Wise after 1521

In Chapter 2 we examined how and why Frederick of Saxony supported and protected Luther in the years leading up to the **Edict of Worms** (1521). In the years that followed, Frederick continued to work tirelessly not just to protect Luther the man, but to promote the religion that Luther stood for.

Frederick was a skilful politician. He used all the advantages of his position to make it difficult for Emperor Charles V to act decisively. He was particularly careful to keep his options open. He always suggested an alternative way forward rather than simply refusing to carry out the wishes of the Emperor. His main tactic was to argue that Luther's ideas needed to be considered more carefully. He suggested that the issue should be decided in Germany at a council of the German Church. This strategy was popular with the German people for two reasons:

- Firstly, the idea itself was appealing. Germans had called for such a council on many occasions in the past, but had been ignored by the Italian-dominated Catholic Church. Frederick was purposely confusing the issue by linking Luther's cause with long-felt national resentments.
- Secondly, the person presenting the idea was one of their most respected leaders who maintained that his aim was the reform of abuses within the Church, not the establishment of an alternative organisation. All the time Frederick presented himself as a reasonable person seeking a reasonable solution, which is essentially what he was.

The role of Charles V

Whilst Frederick's contribution to Luther's cause was great, especially in terms of ensuring that there was sufficient time and space in which it could gain support, there were other causes for Luther's survival. The conflicting priorities of Emperor Charles V were a case in point. In some ways the fact that Charles V ruled over such an extensive but fragmented personal empire, stretching from central Europe to the Americas, was a cause of weakness and not of strength. Even in cases of emergency, he was unable to give his full attention to any one country or issue, let alone tackle the structural defects that made his territories

Key question
Why did Lutheranism spread so rapidly between 1522 and 1530?

Key question
How and why did Frederick the Wise contribute to the spread of Lutheranism after 1521?

Key date
Luther went into hiding after he was outlawed by the Edict of Worms: 1521

Key term
Edict of Worms
The judgement reached by the Diet outlawing Luther and his teachings.

Key question
In what ways was Charles V weakened rather than strengthened by the vastness of his empire?

Emperor Charles V
was out of Germany:
1522–29

Ottoman Empire
Muslim empire
based around
present-day Turkey
whose rapid
expansion
frequently affected
Charles V's handling
of the Lutherans in
Germany.

Key question
Why were the
Catholic princes of
the Empire so
reluctant to help
Charles V deal with
the Lutherans?

almost ungovernable. As a result, Luther was often the least of
his worries. For example:

- Spain: Charles wanted to remain in Germany to ensure that the
  Edict of Worms was carried out, but he was forced to travel to
  Spain to deal with rebellions which had broken out there. He
  was unable to return to Germany for another eight years.
- France: For much of his reign, Charles was also engaged in a
  struggle with France for predominance in European affairs. This
  led to long and costly wars, mainly fought in northern Italy,
  which demanded much of his attention (as we saw in Chapter 5,
  it was the role of the Swiss in these wars that helped to turn
  Zwingli against the Catholic Church).
- The **Ottoman Empire**: Perhaps the biggest issue for Charles was
  the expansion of the Muslim Ottoman Empire. Its sultan,
  Suleiman 'the Magnificent', threatened to dominate the
  Mediterranean and to expand through the Balkans to impinge
  upon Charles's territories in Austria. This meant that Charles was
  forced to compromise with the Lutheran princes in order to win
  their support for the struggle with the Ottoman Empire.

The role of the Catholic princes

Charles was particularly limited by the fact that the princes
questioned his right to interfere in the internal affairs of their
territories within the Empire. The Emperor had not established
the same degree of authority in Germany as the kings of France,
England and Spain had acquired in their kingdoms. And the
territorial rulers of Germany were determined to see that this
situation did not change. So when Charles attempted to act against
those rulers who supported Luther, he found that the Catholic
princes, who should have been his natural allies, were often
lukewarm to his cause. They were both jealous of the ruler's right
to do as he wished within his own territory, and fearful of an
increase in the Emperor's power. They suspected that any army
used to restore the Catholic faith would then be used to impose
Charles's will on all the states of the Empire.

This political division within the ranks of the Catholics ensured
that there would be no speedy resolution of the problem of
Luther. But it did make certain the establishment of a permanent
and separate Lutheran Church. That only happened because
Luther, his supporters and his allies were able to capitalise on the
long breathing space that Frederick the Wise's manoeuvrings and
Charles V's difficulties allowed them.

Profile: Emperor Charles V (1500–1558)

1500 – Born
1506 – Became Duke of Burgundy upon the death of his father
1515 – Became ruler of the Netherlands upon reaching adulthood
1516 – Became King of Spain following the death of his maternal grandfather, Ferdinand of Aragon
1519 – Elected Holy Roman Emperor following the death of his paternal grandfather, Maximilian
1521 – Confronted Luther at the Diet of Worms
1547 – Won a victory against the Protestants at Mühlberg but failed to follow it up
1555 – The Peace of Augsburg acknowledged that the religious divisions in the Empire were permanent
1556 – Abdicated from his Spanish empire in favour of his son, Philip II
1556 – Abdicated from his Habsburg territories and as Holy Roman Emperor in favour of his brother, Ferdinand
1558 – Died in retirement at a Spanish monastery

Charles Habsburg was, in theory at least, one of the most powerful rulers that Europe had ever seen. His paternal grandfather was the Holy Roman Emperor, Maximilian I, through whom Charles inherited large territories in Germany and Austria. Maximilian had married Mary of Burgundy, through whom Charles inherited territories in the Netherlands. His maternal grandparents were just as prestigious, being Ferdinand of Aragon and Isabella of Castile, who together gave Charles control of Spain, Sicily and the Netherlands, not to mention territories in the 'New World'. Finally, in 1519 he was elected Holy Roman Emperor following the death of his grandfather, Maximilian, which meant that his full titles read as follows:

Roman King, future Emperor, semper augustus, King of Spain, Sicily, Jerusalem, the Balearic islands, the Canary islands, the Indies and the mainland on the far shore of the Atlantic, Archduke of Austria, Duke of Burgundy, Brabant, Styria, Carinthia, Carniola, Luxembourg, Limburg, Athens and Patras, Count of Habsburg, Flanders and Tyrol, Count Palatine of Burgundy, Hainault, Pfirt, Rousillon, Landgrave of Alsace, Count of Swabia, Lord of Asia and Africa.

Despite – or perhaps because of – this massive collection of titles and territories, Charles never exerted the sort of influence which might have been expected. Charles had inherited so much territory that he was often left mentally and physically exhausted trying to hold his inheritance together. Mentally, each of his territories had particular issues requiring his involvement, and Charles was rarely able to devote his full attention to any one of them. Physically, he had to spend a great deal of his time travelling between his disparate territories, often in hazardous conditions (his first journey from the Netherlands to Spain saw 160 men drown at sea). It is estimated that he spent about a quarter of his life on the move, and in his abdication speech of 1556 he declared wearily that 'my life has been one long journey'.

Of course, not all of Charles's titles had been inherited. He had actively sought election as Holy Roman Emperor, a role which brought its own problems. As emperor, Charles was expected to defend the Christian faith in a political and military sense whilst the Pope provided religious leadership (the 'doctrine of the two swords'). Charles took this duty very seriously. When he met Martin Luther at the Diet of Worms in 1521, Charles declared his determination to preserve the Catholic faith ('I am determined to set my Kingdoms and dominions, my friends, my body, my blood, my life, my soul upon it'). However, his sense of purpose was not shared by other important figures. Many princes of the Empire adopted Lutheranism; the Catholic princes regarded him as a political rival rather than a religious figurehead; and even the papacy regarded him with suspicion – especially after imperial troops ransacked Rome and forced the Pope to go into hiding (the famous 'Sack of Rome' of 1527).

Charles V is often viewed as something of a failure, the Holy Roman Emperor unable to prevent heresy from sweeping across Germany. The personality of Emperor Charles V played a part. He was shy and awkward, particularly as a young man. He suffered from a protruding 'Habsburg jaw' which affected his speech and meant that he always ate alone. Religiously, he was deeply committed to the Catholic faith (he had been tutored by the future Pope Adrian VI) which made it difficult for him to deal with the Lutherans. Politically, he was rather old-fashioned in his outlook – a man of knightly honour deeply attached to medieval ideas of chivalry. This meant that he was often outmanoeuvred by cynical and unprincipled rulers like Francis I of France (who rejected Charles's demand for a duel in 1528).

Charles himself certainly retired a depressed and broken man. However, he was to a large extent a victim of circumstances which were outside the control of any single individual – Luther included. He failed to achieve his objectives because his objectives were virtually impossible to start with. To his credit, Charles did everything he could to reach a compromise between the Catholics and the Lutherans. He was also hard-working, fair-minded and intelligent. He acquired the ability to speak in several languages to win the support of his subjects (he claimed to speak 'Spanish to God, Italian to women, French to men, and German to my horse').

The role of the Protestant princes and the imperial cities

The survival of Lutheranism was also due to the support gained from a large number of territorial rulers and ruling bodies. It was not merely that they delayed imperial deliberations, which was a vital factor in the years immediately following the Diet of Worms. It was also that they increasingly became totally committed to the Lutheran cause, in a way that Frederick the Wise never did.

The princes

The first prince to take this step was Albrecht of Hohenzollern, Grand Master of the **Teutonic Knights**, who became a Lutheran in 1525. He was followed in 1526 by Philip of Hesse, who was to regard himself as the political leader of the Protestant cause for the next 20 years. Frederick the Wise's successor, John, committed electoral Saxony to Lutheranism in 1527. Other princes followed.

The cities

The number of princes who converted were far outnumbered by the group of imperial cities which became Lutheran by the end of the 1520s. This group contained many of the major trading and wealthy financial centres of Germany. Their prestige and power were considerable. They were generally well able to protect themselves, having city walls that were largely invulnerable to the military technology of the time. There were about 85 imperial cities in total, and over 50 of these became Protestant. With such a solid basis of support, it was clear by the late 1520s that Protestantism could only be destroyed at the cost of a major civil war.

The key debate

In the 1960s, Bernd Moeller expressed concern that historians of the German Reformation were becoming too narrowly concerned with theological issues rather than broader historical questions. The question he posed as a starting point was:

> Why did so many cities turn Protestant?

Moeller's answer to this question was that the appeal of Protestantism was due to the fact that the sense of community in the cities had been eroded in the Middle Ages by the growing power of the imperial government and the papacy. By adopting Lutheranism, the cities were able to reject this authority and re-establish control over their own affairs and to share a common religious life. In particular he focused on the priesthood of all believers, which broke down social barriers and encouraged greater unity.

Steven Ozment, however, stressed that the real reason that the cities adopted the Reformation was religious rather than social. Justification by faith freed the cities from the pyschological burden of good works. He said that the new religious ideas led to social changes, not the other way around. Moreover, far from being a

Key question
How and why did so many princes and imperial cities decide to adopt Lutheranism?

Key term

Teutonic Knights
The Teutonic Knights belonged to one of the military orders that had been established by the Church in the Middle Ages to recapture territory from the pagans who were threatening Christendom from all sides. They had resisted Slav encroachment into eastern Germany and had gained control of part of modern-day Poland.

Key dates

Albrecht of Hohenzollern was converted to Lutheranism: 1525

Philip of Hesse was converted to Lutheranism: 1526

John, Elector of Saxony, was converted to Lutheranism: 1527

movement promoting social unity as Moeller argued, the Reformation was concerned with the personal liberation of each believer from the control of the Church.

Thomas Brady criticised both Ozment's psychological approach and also Moeller's 'romantic conception of urban society' and suggested instead that the Reformation was all about class struggle in which ruling elites in the cities used the Reformation to protect their own vested interests. Using the example of Strasbourg, he said that the ruling classes decided to adopt the Reformation to prevent a popular protest. He suggested that this was likely to be the case in other cities too.

Some key books in the debate:

Bernd Moeller, *Imperial Cities and the Reformation: Three Essays*, reprint (Labyrinth Press, 1982)
Steven Ozment, *The Reformation in the Cities* (Yale University Press, 1975)
Thomas Brady, *Protestant Politics: Jacob Sturm (1489–1553) and the German Reformation* (Humanities Press International, 1995)

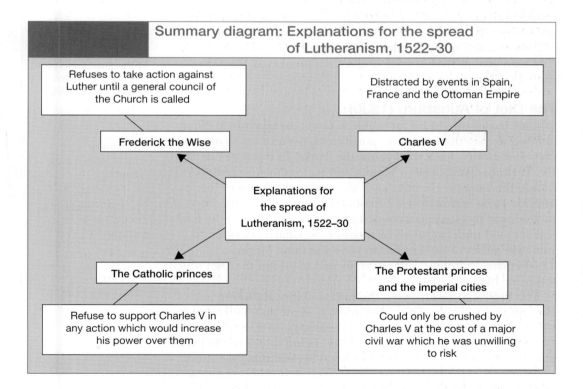

Summary diagram: Explanations for the spread of Lutheranism, 1522–30

Refuses to take action against Luther until a general council of the Church is called

Distracted by events in Spain, France and the Ottoman Empire

Frederick the Wise

Charles V

Explanations for the spread of Lutheranism, 1522–30

The Catholic princes

The Protestant princes and the imperial cities

Refuse to support Charles V in any action which would increase his power over them

Could only be crushed by Charles V at the cost of a major civil war which he was unwilling to risk

3 | Compromise Fails, 1522–30

It is very tempting, with the benefit of hindsight, to assume that the establishment of a totally separate Lutheran Church was inevitable. To most people in the 1520s this was a horrifying prospect. A temporary schism was bad enough. But a permanent schism could create permanent civil conflict which was likely to lead to **anarchy** and the destruction of 'civilised' living.

The Diet of Speyer (1529)

The reformers could not predict the 'when', but they were confident about the 'how'. As the Pope was clearly unprepared to compromise, a council of the Church would have to be summoned. It was generally argued that such a council must be held in Germany, and that delegates should be invited only from Germany. These views were not completely unacceptable to Catholics within the Empire, and negotiations for such a meeting took place between the two groups during the period of Charles's absence from Germany, 1522–29. Only once, at the Diet of Speyer in 1529, did the Catholics attempt to secure the implementation of the Edict of Worms. This led to the representatives of the reformed states making a collective protest against the abandonment of the agreement that no enforcement would take place until after a council had met. The protesters became known as Protestants, a name that has been applied ever since to all Christian groups having their origins in a breakaway from the Catholic Church.

The Diet of Augsburg (1530)

When Charles turned his attention to Germany again in 1530, his aim was to gain the maximum possible support, in terms of both men and money, for a war against the Turks. In the previous year the Turks had laid siege to Vienna and had seemed poised to invade the Empire. He felt that it was essential to present the Muslim Turks with a united Christian front. However, the Pope had refused to summon a council of the Church because he felt that it could undermine his own power. So Charles decided to summon a Diet of the Empire to serve the same purpose. Theologians from both sides were invited to attend the Diet which was to be held at Augsburg.

The Protestants were given the responsibility of finding a compromise solution. They were asked to draw up a statement to which they could all agree, and then to negotiate it with the Catholic representatives. Martin Luther, being under the **imperial ban**, was not able to be present. This was no bad thing for the negotiations, since he had already decided that no compromise could be reached with the Catholics without sacrificing his fundamental beliefs. But some of his leading supporters disagreed. They still hoped to reform the Church of Rome rather than sever links with it altogether.

Key question
Why did the efforts to reconcile Lutherans and Catholics in Germany fail?

Key terms

Anarchy
Chaos, lawlessness. People who promote this state of affairs are called *anarchists*.

Imperial ban
An order such as that imposed on Luther in 1521 which made him an outlaw within the Holy Roman Empire.

Key date

Diet of Speyer: Lutherans 'protested' at the suggestion that the Edict of Worms be enforced: 1529

Profile: Philipp Melanchthon (1497–1560)

1497	– Philipp Schwarzerdt (Greek: *Melanchthon*) was born in Bretten, south Germany, the son of a master of armoury in electoral Saxony
1508	– Taken into the care of his great-uncle, the Hebrew scholar Johann Reuchlin
1509	– Adopted the Greek surname Melanchthon on the advice of his uncle, who believed it sounded more scholarly
1511	– Graduated from Heidelberg University
1514	– Completed his masters degree at Tübingen and began to lecture there on Latin and Greek literature
1515	– Helped to edit *The Letters of Obscure Men,* a humanist attack upon the Catholic critics of Reuchlin
1518	– Appointed professor of Greek at the University of Wittenberg at the age of 21, where he met Luther
1519	– Supported Luther against Johann Eck at the Leipzig Disputations
1521	– Produced the *Loci Communes,* the first systematic statement of Lutheran beliefs
1530	– Authored the Augsburg Confession, which remains the cornerstone of Lutheran theology to this day
1546	– Delivered the oration (speech) at the funeral of Martin Luther
1547	– Bereaved by the death of his daughter and hurt by Protestant accusations that he was soft on Catholicism, he went into semi-retirement
1560	– Died in Wittenberg and was buried next to Martin Luther at the castle church

Philipp Melanchthon was effectively Martin Luther's deputy during the German Reformation. He was professor of Greek at the University of Wittenberg when he met Luther, and they soon became close friends and associates. Melanchthon was a man of great intellect and wide learning. His real surname was 'Schwarzerdt' ('black earth' in German) but as a young man he changed this to its Greek form 'Melanchthon'. By doing this, he was following not only the advice of his guardian, the Hebrew scholar Johann Reuchlin, but also the fashion being set by prominent humanists such as Erasmus.

In general terms, Melanchthon had a great talent for diplomacy which allowed him to present Luther's ideas to both humanists and Catholics as being rational and reasonable. This was partly due to his sincere desire to reach a religious settlement that would re-unite the Christian Church: 'If I could purchase union by my own death,' Melanchthon said, 'I would gladly sacrifice my life.' It was also due, however, to his gentle personality, which won him friends on all sides. Luther himself said of Melanchthon that 'I am rough, boisterous, stormy, and altogether warlike. I must remove stumps and stones, cut away thistles and thorns, and clear the wild forests; but Master Philipp comes along softly and gently sowing and watering with joy, according to the gifts which God has abundantly bestowed upon him.'

Just as Luther brought the Reformation to the common people, Melanchthon's methodical scholarship brought the Reformation to theologians and scholars. Nevertheless, this contrast between the two men should not be overstated. During the Peasants' War of 1524–25, Melanchthon was almost as aggressive as Luther, stating that 'A wild, untamed people like the Germans should not have as much freedom as they presently enjoy … Germans are such an undisciplined, wanton, bloodthirsty people that they should always be harshly governed.'

More specifically, Melanchthon contributed to the Lutheran Reformation in two main ways:

- While Luther was in hiding at Wartburg Castle in 1521, Melanchthon preserved Luther's moderate reforms in Wittenberg against an enthusiastic and radical take-over by the preacher Andreas Karlstadt. He did this by writing the *Loci Communes* (1521), the first clear overview of Luther's main ideas in a systematic form. This book has remained to this day one of the foundations of Protestant thought. The work passed through over 50 editions during his own lifetime. Melanchthon dedicated the 1535 edition of the *Loci* to King Henry VIII, hoping to spread the Reformation to England. Luther was enthusiastic about the book and recommended it as essential reading for understanding his theology.
- Following the failure of the Marburg Colloquy to unite the followers of Luther and Zwingli behind a common statement of belief, Melanchthon wrote the Augsburg Confession (1530). This was a statement of Protestant doctrine addressed to Emperor Charles V and it was designed to unite all Christians in a series of fundamental beliefs. Melanchthon's insistence that good works carried no saving Grace meant that the confession was rejected by the Catholics, whilst its diplomatic vagueness on other issues earned the contempt of hardline Protestants. Nevertheless, to this day it remains the primary statement of belief within the Lutheran Church.

This group of reformers was led by Philipp Melanchthon, who drew up a Protestant statement of beliefs which even left out Luther's cherished idea of a 'priesthood of all believers'. However, despite these efforts to reach out to the Catholics, Luther had been right. The papal representatives were willing to accept compromises from the Protestants but they were not prepared to make any of their own. It quickly became clear that an acceptable agreement could not be reached, and all the Protestant representatives at the Diet withdrew.

Key date

Augsburg Confession: Lutherans drew up a common statement of belief for the first time: 1530

The Augsburg Confession

The breach had not been healed but there had been real gains for the reformers. At last, after several years of trying and failing, a document had been produced that could act as the theological basis for the Lutheran cause. This statement of belief, known as the Augsburg Confession, was clearly the result of many compromises and was deliberately vague in places. But it finally provided a basis for Protestant unity which was desperately needed after Zwingli's debate with Luther at the Marburg Colloquy the previous year. It is regarded as being Melanchthon's finest work, in which he managed to find the words to bridge an almost unbridgeable gap:

> One holy Church will abide for ever. For the Church is the congregation of the saints, in which the gospel is rightly taught and the sacraments are rightly administered. For the true unity of the Church it suffices to agree together concerning the teaching of the Gospel and the administration of the Sacraments; it is not necessary that everywhere should exist similar traditions of men, or similar rites and ceremonies instituted by men ... The body and blood of Christ are really present and are distributed in the Lord's Supper to those who eat; our churches reject those who teach otherwise ... None may publicly teach in church or administer the Sacraments who is not duly called. ... Such are the main heads of our teaching, and in it nothing can be found differing from scripture, or from the Catholic Church, or from the Church of Rome as we understand it from its writers. We are not heretics. Our trouble is with certain abuses that have crept into the Churches without any clear authority. ... The ancient rites are to a large extent carefully preserved among us.

The failure to reach a compromise forced Charles to come out firmly on the side of the Catholics and demand that the Edict of Worms be put into effect. But, although he remained in Germany until 1533, his full attention was on the Turks, and no attempt was made to enforce his authority over the Protestants. He still pinned his hopes on a future Church council despite the fact that the reformers had abandoned their attempt at reconciliation. Certainly they were no longer prepared to consider attending a Church council if it were to be organised and led by the Pope. Yet this was exactly what Charles was trying to arrange.

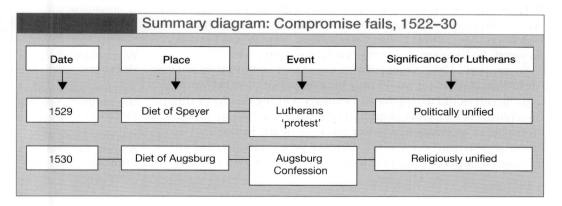

Summary diagram: Compromise fails, 1522–30

Date	Place	Event	Significance for Lutherans
1529	Diet of Speyer	Lutherans 'protest'	Politically unified
1530	Diet of Augsburg	Augsburg Confession	Religiously unified

4 | Protestantism on the Offensive, 1531–40

While there was a realistic hope of reaching an understanding with the Catholic Church, many moderate reformers were reluctant to do anything to aggravate the situation. There was even a widespread feeling that, should the Emperor attempt to enforce the Edict of Worms by military might, he should not be resisted, as to do so would be to challenge the teachings of the Bible. However, following the failure of the Diets of Speyer and Augsburg, the more adventurous leaders of the Protestants were able to take over the leadership of the movement. By far the most powerful of these was Philip of Hesse, who contributed to the spread of Protestantism in Germany in two main ways.

The League of Schmalkalden

Firstly, Philip of Hesse arranged an alliance of most of the important Protestant states in 1531. It was known as the **League of Schmalkalden**, after the town in which the agreement was reached. Although the League was presented as a purely defensive arrangement, it did in fact actively seek to unify and promote Protestant interests. It was remarkably successful in its early years when it seemed as if a new power had emerged in international relations. Charles V, desperate for assistance in 1532 to resist what appeared to be a major offensive by the Turks towards Vienna, was even prepared to agree to suspend all action against members of the League in return for men and money. This agreement, known as the Religious Truce of Nuremberg, persuaded the more nervous Protestant states that it was safe to join the League of Schmalkalden. Ultimately only the city of Nuremberg and the principality of Brandenburg-Ansbach amongst the Protestant territories of Germany did not join the League.

Württemberg becomes Protestant

However, the real triumph was to come in 1534. The large Dukedom of Württemberg (see Figure 3.1, page 57) had been administered by the Habsburgs since 1520 when the Lutheran Duke, Ulrich, had been deposed for murdering a man so he could marry his widow. Philip of Hesse raised an army using money obtained from Francis I of France. This army then marched into Württemberg and restored Ulrich virtually unopposed. Lutheranism became the only religion allowed in the dukedom. The blow to Habsburg and Catholic prestige was serious, especially as Charles accepted the situation and made no attempt to reverse it.

By the mid-1530s, it seemed as if the march of Protestantism was irresistible, and that it would only be a matter of time before Catholicism would disappear in Germany. On the deaths of their rulers in 1535 and 1539, Brandenburg and ducal Saxony became Protestant. The balance of power was now clearly in the Protestants' favour: the Catholic princes were more afraid of an increase in imperial power than they were of reformed religion.

Key questions
What did Protestant rulers in Germany do in the early 1530s in an attempt to strengthen their position? Why were they successful?

Key term

League of Schmalkalden
A military alliance of Lutheran states formed in 1531 and heavily defeated by Charles V at the Battle of Mühlberg in 1547.

Key dates

League of Schmalkalden: Lutherans organised a military alliance: 1531

Württemberg became Protestant: 1534

Joachim, Elector of Brandenburg, became Protestant: 1535

Heinrich, Duke of Saxony, became Protestant: 1539

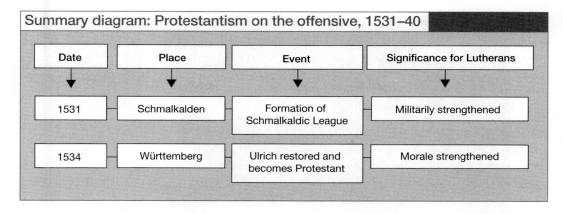

Summary diagram: Protestantism on the offensive, 1531–40

Date	Place	Event	Significance for Lutherans
1531	Schmalkalden	Formation of Schmalkaldic League	Militarily strengthened
1534	Württemberg	Ulrich restored and becomes Protestant	Morale strengthened

Key question
How far was Charles's success against the Protestants between 1541 and 1547 the result of his own skill?

5 | Catholicism on the Offensive, 1541–47

Despite these successes, the Protestants were in a vulnerable position should Charles devote all of his attention and resources to crushing them. They were by no means united, any more than were the Catholics. Many Protestant princes were reluctant to engage in war against the Emperor – even when Luther announced that it was morally right to resist God's appointed ruler provided it was in defence of the teachings in the Bible. So some Protestant states remained outside the League of Schmalkalden, and most of those who were members were likely to put self-interest before the good of the group. It would therefore not be difficult for a skilful manipulator to destroy the fragile alliance.

From 1540, circumstances started turning against the Protestants:

Key dates

Philip of Hesse's reputation was destroyed by a bigamy scandal: 1540

Diet of Regensburg: Charles V decided that military force was needed to crush the Lutherans: 1541

The Ottoman Empire scaled down its European military campaigns. Charles V turned his attention back to the Protestant problem: 1544

Battle of Mühlberg: Charles V defeated the League of Schmalkalden: 1547

- 1540: Philip of Hesse had his reputation destroyed by the scandal of his bigamy (see page 84). This placed him very much at the Emperor's mercy, so the Protestants were virtually leaderless.
- 1541: Charles V once again failed to secure a compromise between the Catholics and the Protestants at the Diet of Regensburg. He finally reached the conclusion that military force was necessary to bring the Lutherans back into the Catholic Church. By this time, the Catholic princes were prepared to support military action against the Protestants, whom they now feared more than a possible extension of imperial power.
- 1544: The Ottoman Empire scaled down its European military campaigns. This meant that Charles V was able to turn his attention back to the Protestant problem.
- 1547: The Battle of Mühlberg ended in complete defeat for the League of Schmalkalden. Its leaders – including Philip of Hesse – were captured. Charles was free to dictate whatever terms he chose. Jubilant at his success, Charles commissioned a famous portrait by Titian which showed him resplendent in battle armour (see page 142).

Portrait of Emperor Charles V at Mühlberg by Titian,1548, Museo del Prado, Madrid, Spain. What message did Charles V aim to send out in this painting?

Summary diagram: Catholicism on the offensive, 1541–47

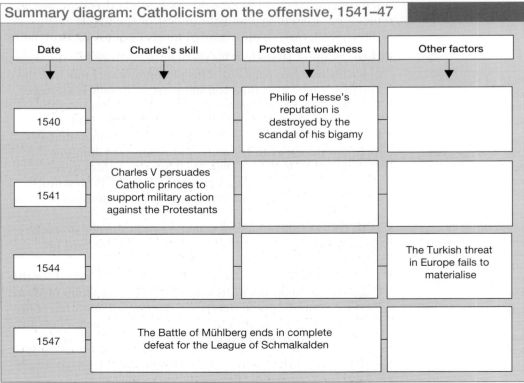

Date	Charles's skill	Protestant weakness	Other factors
1540		Philip of Hesse's reputation is destroyed by the scandal of his bigamy	
1541	Charles V persuades Catholic princes to support military action against the Protestants		
1544			The Turkish threat in Europe fails to materialise
1547	The Battle of Mühlberg ends in complete defeat for the League of Schmalkalden		

Key question
Does Charles V deserve credit for his decision to compromise with the Lutherans after their defeat at Mühlberg?

Key dates

Interim of Augsburg: Charles V proposed moderate religious compromises but these pleased neither Protestants nor Catholics: 1548

Peace of Augsburg: Charles V accepted that the religious divisions in the Empire are permanent: 1555

Key question
What was the significance of the Peace of Augsburg?

6 | Compromise Succeeds, 1548–55

The Interim of Augsburg: 1548

Charles had learnt as a young man the folly of following a major military success with harsh peace terms that leave the defeated party with little alternative but to re-open hostilities. So there were no executions, no seizing of territory by the Habsburgs, and no levying of fines following the Battle of Mühlberg. Instead, Charles attempted to impose a religious settlement on the whole Empire in the form of the Augsburg Interim, a document based on Catholic doctrine, with a few minor modifications designed to give the appearance of compromise with the Lutherans (for example, priests were to be allowed to marry). However, the Interim was almost totally ignored and so in practice Charles's victory had achieved nothing.

Historians have criticised Charles for wasting the one opportunity he had to impose his will on the religious life of Germany. But this judgement is somewhat unfair. His mistake was more in setting himself unrealistic targets rather than in failing to achieve them. By the 1540s it was too late for Lutheranism to be destroyed as an organised religion in most of northern and eastern Germany.

The Peace of Augsburg: 1555

The impossibility of reuniting Christendom was finally recognised in 1555, when at another Diet of Augsburg an agreement was drawn up. This agreement assumed that the schism was permanent, and made arrangements for its management. It was appropriate that Charles was not present at the Diet. He left the arrangements to be made by his brother, Ferdinand, who was soon to take over from him as emperor, while he journeyed to the Netherlands to prepare for the handing over of his other responsibilities to his son, the future Philip II of Spain.

The terms of the so-called Peace of Augsburg remained in force well into the next century and were a clear recognition of the political and religious realities of Germany. In each state there was to be one religion – either Catholicism or Lutheranism. The government of the state was to make the decision. No state was to attempt to force its views on any other state. People were to be free to move, with their belongings, to a state where their religion was practised. This arrangement has been almost universally praised as an example of enlightened good sense and tolerance.

The Peace of Augsburg marked a half-way stage in the Reformation. The early contest had been declared a draw when peace and rest had appeared preferable to continuing struggle and insecurity. On the Protestant side, Luther had been dead for nearly a decade and those of the first generation of reformers who remained alive were old and tired. On the Catholic side, Charles V, who for 30 years had been the driving force behind the efforts to end the schism, was utterly exhausted and retired to a monastery where he devoted his time to maintaining a large collection of clocks. But the battle was far from over: Calvin and his supporters, and the popes of the Counter-Reformation and their supporters, were soon to rekindle the fires of the Reformation.

Portrait of Emperor Charles V Seated by Titian, 1548, Alte Pinakothek, Munich, Germany. Compare this image to the image on page 142, painted in the same year and by the same artist. In what ways does it create a different impression of the Emperor? Which one do you think is the most accurate?

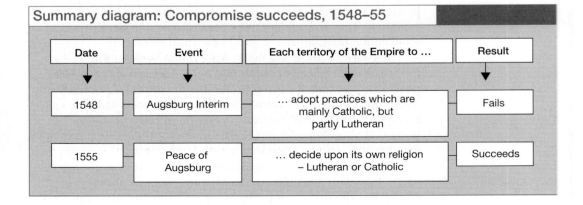

Summary diagram: Compromise succeeds, 1548–55

Date	Event	Each territory of the Empire to …	Result
1548	Augsburg Interim	… adopt practices which are mainly Catholic, but partly Lutheran	Fails
1555	Peace of Augsburg	… decide upon its own religion – Lutheran or Catholic	Succeeds

Study Guide: AS Questions
In the style of Edexcel

To what extent did the failure of Charles V to restore Catholic authority in Germany arise from circumstances beyond his control? (30 marks)

Source: Edexcel Limited specimen material 2007

Edexcel Ltd, accepts no responsibility whatsoever for the accuracy or method of working in the answers given.

Exam tips

The cross-references are intended to take you straight to the material that will help you answer the question.

The question is focused on the extent to which Charles V mishandled his efforts to restore the authority of the Church in Germany. Circumstances beyond Charles's control could include:

- the structure of the Empire and the role of the princes (pages 131, 141)
- the attitude of different popes (pages 135–139) and the failure to compromise
- the size and range of the territory under his control, all of which needed his attention (page 130)
- the extent of the threat from the Turks (pages 131, 140) and the crucial role that played in Charles's decision to suspend actions against the Schmalkalden League
- the difficulties created by France (page 131)
- the role of Frederick the Wise (page 130).

Those matters which Charles could influence included his own priorities, decisions and actions:

- his pursuit of Habsburg interests and his preoccupation with the struggle against the Turks (pages 130–131, 136, 139)
- the negotiations after Mühlberg – how far were these ill-judged (page 143)?

How will you organise these points? What links can you make between them?

In coming to an overall conclusion, take note of the significance of the Religious Truce of Nuremberg (page 140). Did Charles V, in your opinion, have any genuine freedom of action here? And were the consequences of this truce decisive for the authority of the Church in Germany?

In the style of OCR A

Study the five sources on the **Spread of Lutheranism in Germany**, and then answer **both** sub-questions. It is recommended that you spend two-thirds of your time in answering part **(b)**.

(a) Study Sources B and C.
Compare these sources as evidence for the likelihood of war breaking out in Germany. (30 marks)

(b) Study all the sources.
Use your own knowledge to assess how far the sources support the interpretation that Charles V was mainly responsible for the outbreak of war in the 1540s. (70 marks)

The Spread of Lutheranism in Germany
Source A
Valentin von Tetleben, Protokoll des Augsburges, *1530*
Catholic princes in 1530 advise Charles V against war:

Firstly, Charles should know that the sinews of war are money and that he is already in great need of it. Secondly, if the war against the Lutherans and heretics goes badly, the King of France and other rulers will take the opportunity to attack him. Thirdly, if the Turks should by chance make war on the Emperor and Germany, and Germany is in strife and inner turmoil, they will be able to destroy everything within it. Fourthly, unless Charles can gain outside help in the war against the Lutherans, he will not be able to complete it satisfactorily. For if he employs German troops, they could defect from the Emperor to the Lutherans and he might lose his own army. Fifthly, the subjects of the Christian Princes could rebel and rise up against their masters, in which case they would have a war on with their own vassals. For these and other compelling reasons, the Emperor cannot go to war with the Lutherans for the faith.

Source B
Report from Protestant envoys to their town council at Augsburg, June 1541
Augsburg delegates at the Colloquy of Regensburg fear war will soon break out between Charles and the Lutherans:

In the religious discussions, the Emperor dearly wishes progress in those articles which cannot be agreed upon. But our theologians have no wish to participate in more talks and therefore further agreement cannot be expected. I warn you that His Imperial Majesty may perhaps impose his own arrangements. God damn that! Lord Granvelle is mighty angry with the Landgrave of Hesse and ourselves. The Landgrave will in a few days take horse for home. I don't know what will happen then. Granvelle has advised the Landgrave that war is no more than a little finger's breadth away and we should be on our guard.

Source C
Charles, letter to Mary, June 1541
Charles V writes to his sister Mary during the Colloquy of Regensburg:

Unless we take immediate action all the estates of Germany may lose their faith, and the Netherlands may follow. After fully considering all these points, I decided to begin by levying war on Hesse and Saxony [Philip of Hesse and John Frederick of Saxony] as disturbers of the peace, and to open the campaign in the lands of the Duke of Brunswick. This pretext will not long conceal the true purpose of this war of religion, but it will serve to divide the Protestants from the beginning. We shall be able to work out the rest as we go along.

Source D
Report of the Venetian Ambassador, July 1546
The view of a Venetian ambassador at Charles V's court on the situation in Germany:

Concerning the Emperor's disposition towards the States of Germany, every one is at present certain that war is in contemplation. The causes which are said to have moved the Emperor to this are: first, the little regard which the German States have for some years past shown to his orders, by not attending the Diet; and secondly, the fear that the heresy which infects some of them, should spread over them all, and finally pervert his dominions in the Low Countries, which are the chief sources of his greatness. The Princes of Germany have never liked Charles V; probably because he continually avails himself of their counsels, without treating them in the deferential and considerate manner, which Maximilian and all the former Emperors accustomed them to expect.

Source E
M. Rady, The Emperor Charles V, 1988
A modern historian comments on the meeting at Worms between Charles V and the Protestant princes:

The crisis came to a head during the early summer of 1545 when Charles met the Protestant Princes at Worms. They rejected the General Council out of hand, as not being the 'free Christian Council in German lands' they had demanded. Instead, they called for the start of the religious discussions Charles had promised the previous year. Now it was the Princes who were playing for time and, although Charles agreed to their request for talks, he entertained no false hopes. As he recorded in his autobiography, 'the slackness and carelessness which the Princes displayed in this negotiation clearly denoted with what intentions and in what spirit they treated these matters'.

Exam tips

(a) In a comparison of two sources, you must make direct references to the sources themselves, identify any features that are complementary as well as contradictory, and comment on the nature of the sources' authenticity, completeness, consistency, typicality and usefulness. You are not expected to consider all of these qualities but to discuss the most important. Remember that you should only use your own knowledge to provide a context for the sources and your answer should not be driven by contextual knowledge. Some of the main points you might discuss are:

- Both sources were written at the same time and during the Colloquy of Regensburg. Whereas the Augsburg delegates (Source B) feared war would soon occur, Charles V had already decided upon a military solution (Source C).
- Both sources are accurate assessments of the situation though Source B believes that the Emperor does not want war whereas Source C reveals that he now believes he will have to fight.
- The Colloquy was the turning point: Charles genuinely hoped to achieve a peaceful solution, but this has proved unattainable.

(b) The answer requires a good balance between your own knowledge and an analysis of all five sources. Your answer might consider some of the following points:

- Overall the sources suggest the princes, and not Charles, were largely to blame for the break-down in relations.
- Sources B and C hold the Protestant princes responsible, especially Hesse and Saxony; while Source C naturally defends Charles's decision to prepare for war, Source B reflects the view of a Protestant which makes the evidence more compelling.
- Sources D and E hold both Charles and the princes responsible. Charles gave the impression that he was willing to talk but privately suspected the princes of delaying tactics as they prepared for war.
- Source A warned Charles against going to war, advice that was perceptive and largely accurate, but made at a time when only six princes had declared their hand. By 1545 (and arguably as early as 1541) many German states had turned Lutheran, and Charles knew war was unavoidable.

In the style of OCR B

Answer **both** parts of your chosen question.

(a) To what extent did the formation of the Schmalkaldic League mark a real change in the success of Lutheranism in Germany to 1555?

[Explaining events and circumstances]   (25 marks)

(b) Why did Charles V fail to crush the Lutheran advance?

[Explaining actions, events and circumstances]   (25 marks)

Exam tips

Re-read the general introduction in the Exam tips in Chapter 2 (page 44).

(a) This question asks you to explain a pattern: the success of the Lutheran Reformation to 1555. It also gives you the way to do that: by assessing the significance of a possible turning point. You have a 48-year period to cover so stick to the point. Don't structure your answer chronologically. Organise your material by different factors that had a significant impact on Lutheran success.

Because it is suggested within the question, it is essential to start with the League itself. A political and military alliance of states bound to the defence of Lutheranism against the Emperor and Catholic princes was a major breakthrough for the Reformation. But look ahead. While the uneasy peace lasted, the League gave Lutheranism great credibility and the appearance of strength. When put to the test in 1547, however, it failed.

With the given factor now dealt with, consider other possible turning points. Crucially, remember that these turning points can be moments when Lutheranism is weakened as well as strengthened. On this basis, a sensible approach might be to start with all the 'positive' turning points for the Lutherans, e.g. the 1529 Protest, the 1530 Confession, the 1548 Interim – all moments when one or more princes acted decisively. You could then move on to look at some 'negative' turning points: did the death of Luther in 1547 rob Lutheranism of key momentum? Did the 1529 failure of the Colloquy of Marburg rob the young Reformation of a dynamic surge and much strengthened base? Did the 1547 Battle of Mühlberg deliver a terrible blow to Protestant morale?

(b) One line would be to arrange your ideas thematically to different types of reasons. In this respect, the structure of this chapter gives you a great starting point, providing you with details about several key factors including the role of Frederick the Wise, Emperor Charles V, the Catholic princes and the Protestant princes. It makes sense to deal with these in two separate sections: one dealing with the mistakes and weaknesses of the Catholics (Charles V, the Catholic princes) and the other dealing with the strengths and successes of the Protestants (Frederick the Wise, the Protestant princes). You could, if you have time, look into more deep-seated factors: the religious, social, political and cultural grievances of the German people and the ways in which Lutheranism appeared to offer a solution to these problems.

Conclude by addressing which of these factors was the most important. Was Charles V guilty of wasting his opportunity to crush Lutheranism, or were his attempts always doomed to failure? Did Lutheranism win the battle for hearts and minds due to the inherent appeal, or did the Catholics merely lose this battle due to their own mistakes and misjudgements? You do not gain marks for any particular judgement you reach, but what is important is that you attempt to make some sort of judgement rather than simply list a series of factors and then leave the reader to draw a conclusion of their own.

Glossary

Absenteeism   A priest's absence from his parish for long periods of time, neglecting the spiritual welfare of his parishioners.

Abuses   Instances of corruption in the Church.

Ad fontes – **'back to the original'**   The humanist idea of going back to original documents to have a clearer understanding of their true meaning.

Adiophora   Matters of belief and practice which were not considered of central importance.

Agnostic   Someone who refuses either to accept or to deny the existence of God.

Anarchy   Chaos, lawlessness. People who promote this state of affairs are called *anarchists.*

Annales   A school of historians, based in France, who see geographical and climatic conditions as being the main driving force in history.

Annates   A fee paid by a new priest to the papacy, usually amounting to his first year's income. Sometimes known as First Fruits.

Anticlericalism   Opposition to the Church based on its abuse of power and influence.

Atheist   Someone who does not believe in the existence of God.

Bias   A preference for a particular point of view.

Bigamy   The crime of having more than one husband or wife.

Bull   A document containing orders given directly by the Pope in Rome.

Calvin   A second-generation Protestant reformer based in Geneva who focused on issues of organisation as much as belief.

Calvinists   Followers of the reformer John Calvin, who was based in Geneva.

Cannibalism   The act of one human eating the flesh of another.

Canon law   Laws to do with the governance of the Church.

Cantons   The name given to the main administrative districts within Switzerland.

Catechism   A summary of Christian beliefs in the form of short questions and answers.

Chantries   Places where monks would say prayers for souls to help them get into heaven. Many Catholics left money to chantries in their wills.

Charisma   The ability to inspire in others a commitment to a particular point of view.

Christendom   The term used to describe all the territories whose official religion was Christianity.

Christian humanist   A person who applied the techniques of humanism to the Christian Scriptures to get closer to the original meaning.

Christocentric realism   An artistic style which encouraged Christians to focus more on the teachings of Christ through a realistic depiction of his life and crucifixion.

City-state   A city which runs its own affairs and is subject to no outside authority.

Civil war   A war between people of the same nationality.

Confederation   A form of government in which national decisions are taken by a central government and local decisions are made at a lower level.

Congregation   A group of people who attend the same church.

Consubstantiation   Luther's idea that Christ's body and blood are absorbed into, rather than replace, the bread and the wine during the ceremony of the Eucharist.

Council   The elected governing body of Zurich. The council claimed control over all aspects of life, including religion.

Curia   The government and civil service of the papacy in Rome.

Damnation   The state of being condemned to everlasting punishment in hell.

The Damned   People whose souls were destined to go to hell.

Devotio Moderna   Literally 'modern devotion' – a Catholic movement based in Holland which stressed that a simple devotion to the teachings of Christ was more important than carrying out rituals.

Edict of Worms   The judgement reached by the Diet outlawing Luther and his teachings.

The Elect   The group of people who had been marked out by God as being destined for heaven.

Elector   One of the seven princes who elected the Holy Roman Emperor.

Electoral Saxony   The state within the Holy Roman Empire where Luther began his protest. A generation earlier the state of Saxony had been divided in two – electoral Saxony ruled over by an elector, and ducal Saxony ruled over by a duke.

Evangelical   Describing a Bible-based religion which focuses heavily on sermons and preaching rather than rituals and ceremonies.

Excommunication   The act of casting someone out of the Church, resulting in their being destined for hell.

Fasting   The religious practice of abstaining from food to bring oneself closer to God.

Figuratively   Symbolically or metaphorically.

Good works   Worthy actions such as charity work and pilgrimages. Catholics believe these help a soul to get into heaven.

Grace   Merit in the eyes of God. A 'state of Grace' is a condition of perfection which allows a soul to enter into heaven.

Habsburg   The powerful royal family to which Emperor Charles V belonged and which controlled Spain and the Netherlands; it also controlled much of Italy, Germany and Austria.

Holy relics   Artefacts from the life of a saint – bones, hair, clothing and so on – which were felt by Catholics to have special powers to heal and bestow Grace.

Holy Roman Emperor   The leader of the Holy Roman Empire, which was a loose confederation of states roughly equating to modern-day Germany, Austria, Hungary and the Netherlands.

Humanists   The followers of an intellectual movement which encouraged people to read original texts for themselves rather than accept the interpretations of others.

Hussites   Medieval heretics based in Bohemia who followed the teachings of Jan Huss.

Iconoclasm   The Protestant process of stripping churches of images of saints.

Idealistic   More concerned with ideals than with practical realities.

Imperial ban   An order such as that imposed on Luther in 1521 which made him an outlaw within the Holy Roman Empire.

Imperial cities   Places in the Holy Roman Empire which were not under the control of a particular prince and which represented themselves at the Imperial Diet.

Imperial Diet   The parliament of the Holy Roman Empire. This met in various cities around the Empire during this period, including Worms, Augsburg and Speyer.

Imperial Knights   A class of minor nobles in the Holy Roman Empire.

Impunity   Freedom from punishment of any kind.

Italian Wars   A series of conflicts in which various Italian states, allied with either the French or the Habsburgs, tried to dominate the others.

Justification   The process by which a soul justifies (explains) why it is worthy of entering heaven.

Laity   A general term referring to Christian people who were not ordained priests. A person within this group would be described as a layperson or a layman.

League of Schmalkalden   A military alliance of Lutheran states formed in 1531 and heavily defeated by Charles V at the Battle of Mühlberg in 1547.

Liberalism   A political philosophy that champions individual freedoms and personal rights.

Literally   Based on the direct meaning of words.

Literate   Able to read. People unable to read are described as being *illiterate*.

Lollards   Medieval heretics based in England who followed the teachings of John Wycliffe.

Magisterial Reformation   The idea that the Reformation should be led by responsible officials such as magistrates and princes rather than by the common people.

Martyr   Someone who dies in defence of their religious beliefs.

Marxist   A follower of Karl Marx, a highly influential nineteenth-century historian and philosopher who saw economic factors as being the main driving force in history.

Mass   The central sacrament of the Catholic Church re-enacting the Last Supper, when bread and wine become the body and blood of Jesus Christ.

Mercenaries   Soldiers for hire. Because the Swiss had so little agricultural land, they hired out mercenaries to raise money to pay for grain.

Missionaries   People who attempt to convert others to a particular religious faith.

Nationalist   Someone who vigorously defends and promotes their country's language, culture and outlook.

Nepotism   The practice of giving jobs to people who are friends and family members rather than employing the most talented.

Notorious   Famous for all the wrong reasons.

Original sin   The 'first crime' – in the Old Testament, Adam and Eve were thrown out of the garden of Eden when Eve disobeyed God by eating the 'forbidden fruit' (an apple).

Orthodox   The established version of the truth.

Ottoman Empire   Muslim empire based around present-day Turkey whose rapid expansion frequently affected Charles V's handling of the Lutherans in Germany.

Papacy   A term referring to the Catholic institution consisting of the Pope and his close advisers.

Papal estates   The extensive territories belonging to the Pope within Italy.

Patron saint   A holy figure associated with a particular trade. Luther's patron saint was St Anne, the patron saint of miners.

Pilgrimages   Journies to holy places such as Jerusalem. Catholics regard pilgrimages as an example of 'good works'.

Pluralism   The practice of holding several jobs in the Church in order to become wealthy.

Pope   The leader of the Catholic Church. This was Leo X when Luther's protest began.

Pragmatic   More concerned with practical realities than with ideals.

Predestination   The idea that God, being all-knowing and all-powerful, has already decided which souls are going to heaven and which souls are going to hell.

Prejudice   Very fixed opinions.

Priesthood of all believers   Luther's idea that everyone, given access to the Bible, could effectively become his own priest.

Propaganda   A form of advertising designed to persuade people to view things in a certain way.

Protestant   A general term referring to anyone who 'protested' against the Catholic Church.

Radical   From the Latin word for 'root'. A point of view which is regarded as being extreme and outlandish.

Radicals   A general term referring to extreme Protestants who felt that the Lutheran Reformation was too moderate.

Rational   Taking a logical and scientific approach.

Rebel   Someone who questions an existing system of belief and/or government.

Reform   Change for the better. The term 'Reformation' is therefore one that has inbuilt bias.

Renaissance   The 'Rebirth' of classical learning in the late medieval period which encouraged people to think for themselves rather than blindly accept what they were told.

Revolutionary   Someone who aims to overthrow an existing system of belief and/or government.

Roman See   The Bishopric (See) of Rome – another word for the papacy.

Sacraments   The central rituals of the Catholic Church, administered by a priest, which were essential for salvation.

Safe conduct   A promise that no harm will come to someone if they agree to travel to meet someone.

St Thomas Becket   An archbishop of Canterbury who was murdered after defending the Church against the King of England.

Salvation   The process of being saved from the flames of hell through God's forgiveness.

Schism   A division or a split within a group or an organisation.

Scholasticism   A medieval intellectual movement which focused on adding increasing layers of detail and analysis onto original texts to provide an ever-deepening body of understanding.

Scribe   A monk whose job was to produce copies of books by hand. They played an essential role in recording and spreading knowledge before the invention of the printing press.

Scriptures   The sacred written texts of the Christian faith.

Second Coming   The return of Christ to earth on the day of the Last Judgement, when all souls will finally be granted entry into heaven or cast into hell for all eternity.

Secular   To do with worldly, political affairs rather than those to do with religion.

Sermons   Speeches given by priests on matters of religion.

Simony   The practice of selling jobs in the Church to the highest bidder rather than the best qualified.

Sin   A crime against the laws of God – for example breaking one of the Ten Commandments.

Skirmish   A minor clash between two opposing military forces.

Sola scriptura   'By scripture alone' – the idea that any church beliefs and practices not outlined in the Bible did not help a soul enter heaven.

Spiritualists   A group of extreme Protestants who rejected the Bible in favour of direct communication with God through prayer.

Swiss Brethren   A group of radical reformers based in Zwingli's Zurich who argued that only adults could be baptised. Sometimes known as 'Anabaptists'.

Teutonic Knights   The Teutonic Knights belonged to one of the military orders that had been established by the Church in the Middle Ages to recapture territory from the pagans who were threatening Christendom from all sides. They had resisted Slav encroachment into eastern Germany and had gained control of part of modern-day Poland.

Theology   The study of religion, in particular the relationship between God and humanity. Its students are known as theologians.

Tithe   A tax paid by parishioners to their priest of ten per cent of their annual income.

Transubstantiation   The Catholic idea that the bread and the wine are physically transformed into the body and blood of Christ during the ceremony of the Eucharist.

Tyranny   An evil dictatorship. The person in charge of such a regime is described as a *tyrant*.

Veneration   Extreme respect for a person or an object.

Vengeance   The act of taking revenge.

Vernacular   The language of the people. Luther argued that the Bible should be in the vernacular rather than in Latin.

Vestments   The ceremonial clothing worn by Catholic priests.

Vulgate   The centrally approved Latin Bible of the Catholic Church.

Woodcuts   Images carved into wood and printed onto paper.

Zwickau Prophets   A group of radical reformers who campaigned for the physical destruction of images within churches.

Zwinglians   Followers of the reformer Ulrich Zwingli, who was based in Zurich (see Chapter 5).

Index